Spiritual Transformation

Spiritual Transformation

Taking on the Character of Christ

Richard Peace

WIPF & STOCK · Eugene, Oregon

SPIRITUAL TRANSFORMATION
Taking on the Character of Christ

Copyright © 2016 Richard Peace. All rights reserved. Except for brief quotations in critical publications or reviews, no part of this book may be reproduced in any manner without prior written permission from the publisher. Write: Permissions, Wipf and Stock Publishers, 199 W. 8th Ave., Suite 3, Eugene, OR 97401.

Wipf & Stock
An Imprint of Wipf and Stock Publishers
199 W. 8th Ave., Suite 3
Eugene, OR 97401

www.wipfandstock.com

PAPERBACK ISBN: 978-1-4982-3156-5
HARDCOVER ISBN: 978-1-4982-3158-9

Manufactured in the U.S.A.   OCTOBER 11, 2016

For David R. Nelson
friend, colleague, collaborator, and all-around good guy
for more years than I can remember

Contents

How to Use this Guide | ix
An Introduction to Spiritual Transformation | xiii

Session One
    The Process of Transformation | 1

Session Two
    The Renewing of Our Minds | 13

Session Three
    Insight | 25

Session Four
    Knowing Ourselves | 35

Session Five
    Repentance | 45

Session Six
    Loving Others | 53

Session Seven
    Confession | 65

Session Eight
    Service Not Retaliation | 75

Session Nine
    Faith | 85

Session Ten
    Citizenship | 95

Session Eleven
    Community | 107

Session Twelve
    Love in the Last Days | 115

Leader's Notes for this Study | 129
Bibliography | 149

How to Use This Guide

Transformation is what Christianity is all about. To follow Jesus is to enter into a journey from an old way of living to a new way of being. As Christians our goal is to become ever more conformed to the image of Christ. Of course we cannot attain this high goal in our lifetime. But we can make progress. We can become more of who we long to be. We can leave behind old ways that have not served us well. We can become more loving to others, more open to God, more in tune with who we are called to be.

Such transformation does not happen automatically, even though it is the Holy Spirit working in us to change us. We are asked to "to work out your own salvation with fear and trembling; for it is God who is at work in you, enabling you both to will and to work for his good pleasure" (Phil 2:12–13). We work; God works in us. This book is about our part in the work of transformation.

What's it all about?

This is a study guide that will help you explore what growth and change is all about in the Christian life. Our goal as Christians is to become ever more like Jesus in how we think, feel, and act. This sort of transformation can and does happen (even though at times such change seems out of reach to us).You can use this guide on your own, or better still, with a small group of like-minded people.

Who is this small group program for?

Anyone who longs to live a God-oriented life, anyone who is tired of staying in the same spot spiritually, and anyone who wants to become more whole (holy).

How to Use This Guide

What will we study?

There are two parts to the course. Six sessions focus on the *dynamics of transformation*: what it is, how it happens, and what elements bring it about. During these sessions, you are invited to work on a particular issue that is of concern to you.

The other six sessions focus on the *goal of transformation*: what it is that we are called to become as we seek to be conformed to the image of Christ. These sessions focus on Romans 12 and 13 where St. Paul provides a blueprint for how we are meant to live.

What will I learn?

You will come to understand the process of transformation and how, potentially, to open yourself to this process as a normal part of your life.

You will come to understand the core ideas, attitudes, and actions that are meant to characterize our lives as followers of Jesus.

Is this course only for church people goers?

No, it is for anyone who is hungry to know God. The material is written from a Christian point of view and the way of life that is described is drawn from the New Testament. However this does not mean that you have to be a follower of Jesus to explore this way of life. In fact, this course will give you the opportunity to reflect on the Christian Way and, we hope, to make a decision to follow Jesus.

But what if I do not know much about the Bible?

No problem. We will use two translations of the New Testament to aid comprehension. The *New Revised Standard Version* (NRSV) translation is more literal and *The Message* is a modern paraphrase. The Bible study questions are designed to help you penetrate the meaning of the text. In addition there are Bible study notes for each passage. These notes give you background information about the passage (*Context*) and suggestions as to how the passage might apply to your life (*Connection*).

After the small group series ends, you will have mastered two important chapters from the book of Romans and you be on your way to becoming knowledgeable about the Bible.

How to Use This Guide

Can I do this course without a small group?

Yes. Rather than answering the questions as part of a group conversation, keep a journal and write out your responses as a way of reflection.

What will a group do for me that I can't do on my own?

Given our busy schedules, it is a challenge to explore such matters on our own. We need a small group of like-minded people who meet together on a regular basis in order to have the energy and the motivation to study, not to mention the valuable input from others as we wrestle together with these ideas.

And the fact is that we were never meant to grow on our own. The Christian way is a community way. We need others and others need us if we are to get on with this business of becoming all God wants us to be.

How long is this course?

There are twelve small group sessions. The best way to cover this material is to meet together once a week.

However, since there are two types of small group sessions, if time is a problem you might want to meet for only six weeks. You could do the six Bible studies that examine the nature of the Christian life. Or you could do the six discussion sessions that examine the dynamics of transformation.

You might decide to do the discussion sessions together in the small group and then assign the Bible studies as homework. This would take only six weeks.

How long is each session?

Ninety minutes is the ideal length of time for each small group session. However, you can cover the material in sixty minutes by omitting some of the questions.

If you are working on your own, each session will take less time. But, of course, this depends on you. Many people have found that writing reflections in a journal can be a very intense process.

Who leads the meeting?

Anybody can serve as a small group leader. There are notes at the end of the book that describe what the leader needs to know and do. However, like anything else, the more experienced the leader the better. If you have an experienced small group leader, take advantage of his or her skills.

What kind of commitment is involved?

You will need to make attendance at each small group session a priority. Your presence will be missed if you are absent. And the material unfolds in an orderly sequence with each session building on the previous sessions.

How do I recruit members for this small group?

All it takes to start a group is the willingness of one person to make some phone calls. Describe to potential group members what this course is all about. Ask them to phone their friends to join. Before you know it you will have four to twelve others and another small group is born. (The optimum size for a small group is between 5 and 13 people.)

An Introduction to Spiritual Transformation

I HAVE LONG BEEN interested in the process of transformation. Much of my academic work has focused on the question of how people grow and change. In particular, I have been fascinated by the phenomenon of conversion. Conversion is, of course, an example of transformation.[1] In this book what I have tried to do is to share some of what I have learned about transformation, expressed in the format of a study guide to be used by individuals and small groups which seek to grow and change.

The Call to Transformation

It is this ability to grow and change that makes us human. After all, it is God who has created us in such a way that transformation is possible. No other living species is like us in this regard. For example, a bear is always a bear. He lives his whole life guided by innate instincts. Sure, he can learn new "tricks" like you see in the circus but this is just a mild alteration of his existing behavioral patterns. But the bear remains the same bear he always was.

But human beings are not locked into an unchanging set of patterns. We can change from the inside out. We can shed our old natures and take on new ones. We can stop in mid-stream, turn around from the direction our lives have been taking, and go in a completely new direction. This is really quite astonishing when you think about it. We should be profoundly grateful to God that we are not forced to live pre-determined lives within the narrow boundaries of genetic and instinctual givens. We can become new creatures in Christ.

St. Paul puts it this way, "You were taught to put away your former way of life, your old self, corrupt and deluded by its lusts, and to be renewed in

---

1. See my book *Conversion in the New Testament*, 1999.

the spirit of your minds, and to clothe yourselves with the new self, created according to the likeness of God in true righteousness and holiness" (Eph 4:22–24). In another place Paul says, "Do not lie to one another, seeing that you have stripped off the old self with its practices and have clothed yourselves with the new self, which is being renewed in knowledge according to the image of its creator" (Col 3:9–10).

My fascination with the transforming process led to my interest in spiritual formation (and Christian spirituality in general). Some years ago I wrote four books on the spiritual disciplines.[2] The aim of the various spiritual disciplines is to induce and sustain change in the direction of God. This book completes the *Spiritual Disciplines Study Guide* series. In this book I step back from a consideration of individual means by which such change is induced (such as spiritual journaling, spiritual autobiography, prayer, and encounter with the Bible) and examine the foundational question, namely, what is the dynamic of change itself?

This is no mere academic study, however. What I have tried to do is create a resource that both examines the process of spiritual change and creates an environment within which such change can actually take place. As I will be arguing, such change involves individual work and awareness, a small group environment which encourages and helps sustain growth, and, of course, the grace of God and the work of the Holy Spirit. This book provides material for individual reflection and a guide for an ongoing small group experience.

The Mystery of Transformation

I do not mean to suggest, however, that there is some sort of magic formula that automatically makes princes and princesses out of toads and frogs. Nor do I want to suggest that this process is completely in our control. In fact, it is not in our control. But what we can do is to put ourselves in the places where growth can occur, recognizing that the inner work of growth is the job of the Holy Spirit.

You see, transformation touches upon a central mystery of the Christian faith, namely, that we are to "continue to work out [our] salvation with fear and trembling for it is God who works in [us] to will and to act according to his good purpose" (Phil 2:12–13, NIV). It is both God and

---

2. Peace, *Spiritual Journaling, Spiritual Autobiography, Contemplative Bible Reading,* and *Meditative Prayer.*

An Introduction to Spiritual Transformation

us. It is God working in us and it is we working at growth. Change is our responsibility. Change is God's responsibility. Both are true simultaneously. This is a mystery.

Later on in the same letter Paul tells us, "Join with others in following my example, brothers [and sisters] and take note of those who live according to the pattern we gave you" (Phil 3:17, NIV). This is our side of the equation. There is a pattern. We can know it. We can work at living in accord with it. But then Paul ends this paragraph by assuring us that "the Lord Jesus Christ, who, by the power that enables him to bring everything under his control, will transform our lowly bodies so that they will be like his glorious body" (Phil 3:20–21, NIV). In these verses Paul has in mind the final resurrection when we will be given transformed bodies. This is God's side of the equation. Transformation is brought about by the work of Christ. This is a mystery.

At the heart of transformation is the awareness of who we truly are in the eyes of God. When we know that we are a son or daughter of God we live life quite differently. The discovery of this fact is often the first step in the path of transformation. The name for this step is *conversion*. Conversion is a profound form of transformation whereby we stop living in the world of darkness (as Paul defines it in Romans 13) and start living in the world of light (where God is). Conversion is all about turning from our own ways (which are ultimately destructive) to Jesus (who calls us to a new way). As we will see, the dynamics of conversion (repentance and faith) are also the dynamics of all transformation. Your call during this small group series may be to conversion to Jesus.

The Structure of the Book

The book, *Spiritual Transformation*, consists of two types of study material: a reflection on the dynamics of transformation and a study of Romans 12 and 13 where Paul describes for us what it means to live as a follower of Jesus. Each strand is approached in a somewhat different fashion.

In the six sessions that examine the anatomy of transformation, there is a *Consider* section that consists of input on a particular aspect of transformation. (It is best if each person reads this material before coming to the group but you can take time to read it silently during the session if you wish.) The *Discussion* section generates a conversation that focuses on what has been presented in the *Consider* material. This, then, leads into the *Application* section, which gives you a chance to discuss how these ideas connect with everyday life.

In the six sessions of Bible Study you first read *The Passage* (in two translations of the New Testament) and then engage in *Analysis* of the passage. The session moves then to *Application*, which seeks to connect what the Bible is saying to how we are living. The Bible Study sessions end with *Bible Study Notes* on the passage that help you understand the text in its original *Context* and then make *Connections* to everyday life.

Each session in both strands of material is prefaced by an *Overview* that will give you a sense of what will be covered in that particular session followed by a *Unison Prayer* as a way to pray as a group. The session then moves to an *Open* exercise. This is what is called a history-giving exercise in which you each share, briefly, stories from your own experience that focus on the main topic of the session. This is fun way to begin, to get to know one another, and to start thinking about the topic. Each session ends with a time of group *Prayer* around various topics you have considered, followed by *Reflection* questions to be used during the week between sessions. This reflection works best if you use a journal and write out your thoughts.

Sources

In the 1980s I produced a series of notes on the book of Romans.[3] I have used the insights from that project to develop the Bible studies on Romans in this book. At that time the short book by John Stott on Romans 5-8 (*Men Made New*) proved most insightful. Later Stott produced a commentary on the whole of Romans (*Romans: God's Good News for the World*) that is superb in the clarity it brings in understanding the text. (This is what we have come to expect from Stott.) I have made good use of his book (as the footnotes will indicate), as well as the other standard critical tools and commentaries on Romans, in particular *A Critical and Exegetical Commentary on the Epistle to the Romans* by C.E.B. Cranfield, *The Epistle to the Romans* by C. K. Barrett, *Wrestling with Romans* by John A. T. Robinson, and *The Epistle of Paul to the Romans* by F. F. Bruce.

3. Peace & Coleman, *Study Guide for the Book of Romans* and *Pastor/Teacher Commentary for Romans* in the *Mastering the Basics* series.

An Introduction to Spiritual Transformation

Acknowledgments

I appreciate the help I have been given on this project. I owe a debt of gratitude to my students, especially those in the Christian Spirituality track of the Doctor of Ministry program at both Gordon-Conwell Theological Seminary and Fuller Theological Seminary. We discussed together my paradigm for transformation and I benefited greatly from their insights. Throughout this whole series my wife Judy has been a presence. Not only has she offered a host of insights but also she has helped to create the environment in which I have written. Most especially, she has been the person who has walked with me in my own struggles to "get it right" in my own life.

I am more convinced than ever that the core challenge of the Christian life is to hear God in God's many voices.[4] To say that God is alive and personal is more than mere theological rhetoric. This is meant to be a daily reality for each of us. And yet it is so hard to notice God. There are so many other, competing voices. We are often deaf to God's voice (which is mostly soft and gentle). We are often blind to God's presence (which is all around us). We need to work at hearing and seeing. The spiritual disciplines are simply the vehicles through which we learn to hear and to see. May God grant all of us new ears and new eyes as our lives are being transformed so that we become vibrant members of God's kingdom into which we (and all people) have been so graciously invited.

I invite you into the adventure of transformation. May this small group be much more than just another interesting conversation amongst people of like-concern. May this be, literally, life-transforming.

---

4. See my book *Noticing God*.

SESSION ONE

The Process of Transformation

The Nature and Character of Transformation

OVERVIEW

In order to explore the dynamics of transformation it is important to understand what is meant by transformation and how transformation occurs. This first session focuses on a paradigm by which to understand the process of transformation. The details of this paradigm will then be examined in the following sessions.

Unison Prayer

Pray together a prayer from St. Anselm (1033–1109) which expresses the confidence that one day fullness will be his (and our) experience.

> *My God,*
> *I pray that I may so know you and love you*
> *that I may rejoice in you.*
> *And if I may not do so fully in this life,*
> *let me go steadily on*
> *to the day when I come to that fullness . . .*
> *Let me receive*
> *That which you promised through your truth,*
> *that my joy may be full. Amen.*[1]

---

1. Appleton, *Oxford Book of Prayer*, 66.

SPIRITUAL TRANSFORMATION

OPEN   20–30 MINUTES
Transforming Moments

We all have them: encounters or experiences as a result of which the texture of life shifts on us. At such times we become new people in some way, big or small. Reflect on some of your childhood experiences as a way of introducing yourself to the other group members.

1. Introduce yourself to the group by briefly describing the world in which you presently live:

   - Who you live with
   - What you do with most of your day
   - How you nurture the spiritual side of life

2. Which was the most traumatic moment of change for you when you were young?

   ❏ the discovery of Santa's true nature
   ❏ the discovery that you actually have to go to school
   ❏ the discovery that you were in love
   ❏ the discovery that God exists
   ❏ the discovery that you were not the center of the universe
   ❏ the discovery that you got graded for your work in school
   ❏ the discovery that you actually had to share
   ❏ the discovery that the Easter Bunny (or tooth fairy) is not what you thought
   ❏ the discovery that _____

3. Give one reason why you joined this small group.

CONSIDER 15–20 MINUTES

The Experience of Transformation

The word *transformation* has an exotic ring to it. It conjures up images of hairy caterpillars suddenly emerging as graceful butterflies, of ugly ducklings turning into beautiful swans, of cursing drunks becoming gentle caregivers, and of a clumsy scullery maid like Cinderella discovering that she is actually a beautiful princess.

We like the whole idea of transformation. We want it to happen to us. How wonderful it would be if all our ugliness, hesitation, and bewilderment turned into beauty, confidence, and wisdom. And how great if this happened magically. Poof! A fairy godmother waves a wand and you are transformed.

Guess what? This *does* happen in real life. We all know stories of sudden transformation:

- The alcoholic aunt who stumbles through life never far from a bottle until one day she wakes up, realizes her life has bottomed out, goes to an AA meeting, meets God there who becomes her higher power, and never drinks again.

- Or what about the rake who, for distorted reasons of his own, has ruined the lives of more than one person, and then he finds Christ via a grubby tract pushed into his hand one day and he becomes a minister of the gospel who brings new life to countless others.

- Then there is Peter who on one day is denying Christ ("I don't even know the man") and a few days later he is defying the Sanhedrin ("I don't care what you do to me. I know Jesus is risen from the dead").

- And what about St. Paul? One day he is breathing murderous threats against Christians. But then the resurrected Jesus stops him in his tracks and makes him into the apostle to the Gentiles who brought Christianity to the West (from which the church we participate in twenty-one centuries later emerged).

This is the good news, really good news. Sudden transformation can and does happen. It has probably even happened to you at some point in your life.

But this is not the whole story. The bad news is that sudden transformation, alas, is the exception, not the rule. Mostly growth and change comes slowly and in small increments. We cannot "order up" rapid transformation from a celestial menu, as it were. But in fact, this is not really bad news. It is just different news. The important thing is that we can be transformed, albeit in a slower fashion.

And even for those who, in a moment, get stopped in their tracks, turned around from a destructive lifestyle, and launched into a new life of service, there is still a lot of hard work ahead. Take St. Paul for example. Sure, Jesus' powerful presence and penetrating question enabled him to reevaluate the meaning of his whole life. But Paul still had to spend years in the desert working out what had actually happened to him and then letting his new life in Christ re-make him on a deep level. Transformation can be instantaneous but it is never complete all at once. Once we have been turned around and started in a new direction the work begins. The real challenge is to make transformation—or change—a regular part of everyday life.

The Call to Transformation

How can we develop a lifestyle that brings about transformation? The first step is to recognize that we are called to live this sort of life. In becoming a follower of Jesus we are signing on to a life of growth and change. And our goal is clear: to become like Jesus.

And our challenge is also clear: we are far from what we ought to be in thought, attitude, and deed. We need transformation. We are flawed, distorted, and incomplete. On one level we cannot help this state of affairs. It is just the way human beings are and it has to do with the fact that our ancient ancestors chose against God and so a flawed gene, as it were, entered the human race and has yet to be wiped out. (The theological term for this is "original sin.") But this is not the whole story. We ourselves continue to choose, on a regular basis, not to live in God's way. We are not merely passive victims of our ancestor's misdeeds. We make our own mistakes all the time both by what we do and what we fail to do.

We need transformation. That much is clear.

And the Bible urges us to be transformed. It does so in various ways:

- In Mark 1:17 Jesus says to the four fisherman (Peter, Andrew, James, and John), "Follow me." This is the most basic call of all, a call to a life of transformation. When we start to follow Jesus, we start on the path of transformation. Over the course of time we will become quite different from whom we were when we first said "Yes" to Jesus.

- In Romans 12:2 Paul calls us to the "renewing of [our] minds." He says that we must leave behind our conformity to this world which has hitherto shaped our lives and instead be "transformed" as our thinking is brought more and more into conformity with God's thinking. This is transformation of our worldview, our way of thinking, and our lifestyle.

- In Ephesians 4:22–24 St. Paul uses a metaphor of clothing to describe the call to transformation. We are to strip off old, ragged, filthy garments and put on fresh, clean clothes. What we strip off is our old nature with its "deceitful desires" and what we put on is the new nature of Christ. "Put on the new self created to be like God in true righteousness and holiness." This is a call to be transformed inside and out.

The Goal of Transformation

The goal of transformation is not difficult to discern. It is written across the pages of the New Testament. The goal of transformation is to be *conformed to the image of Christ*. It is to be like Christ. It is to open us to the mind of Christ. It is to let Christ reign in our lives.

Listen to the various ways in which the New Testament speaks of this reality:

- "For those whom [God] foreknew he also predestined to be conformed to the image of his Son . . . " (Rom 8:29).

- "And just as we have borne the likeness of the earthly man, so shall we bear the likeness of the man from heaven" (1 Cor 15:49, NIV).

- "And all of us, with unveiled faces, seeing the glory of the Lord as though reflected in a mirror, are being transformed into the same image from one degree of glory to another; for this comes from the Lord, the Spirit" (2 Cor 3:18).

The Power for Transformation

But what makes such transformation possible? The New Testament tells us that what makes transformation possible is the fact that *we are in Christ and Christ is in us*. The aim of transformation is to become, in reality, what we already are, in fact: bearers of the image of Christ. And it is the living Christ that brings this about.

- "I have been crucified with Christ; and it is no longer I who live, but it is *Christ who lives in me*. And the life I now live in the flesh I live by faith in the Son of God, who loved me and gave himself for me" (Gal 2:19–20).
- "To them God chose to make known how great among the Gentiles are the riches of the glory of this mystery, which is *Christ in you*, the hope of glory" (Col 1:27).
- "For who has known the mind of the Lord so as to instruct him? But *we have the mind of Christ*" (1 Cor 2:16).
- "Do you not realize that *Christ Jesus is in you* . . . ?" (2 Cor 13:5).
- "I pray that, according to the riches of his glory, he may grant that you may be strengthened in your inner being with power through his Spirit, and that *Christ may dwell in your hearts* through faith, as you are being rooted and grounded in love" (Eph 3:16–17).

The Process of Transformation

So how does transformation work? As a beginning definition, think of the process of transformation in terms of the *image of turning*. You are going in one direction, the wrong direction. You discover that the path you are taking leads away from God. So you stop, turn around, and start going the opposite direction, which is toward God. This is Christian transformation. It involves five aspects:

1. *Insight*: The realization that I am going in the wrong direction when it comes to how I think, feel, or act. I realize that the path on which I am walking is taking me away from God not toward God.
2. *Repentance*: The next step is to decide that I do not want to go in that direction any longer. I decide to turn around and go in God's direction.

3. *Confession*: The decision to turn around involves acknowledging to appropriate others that I have decided to change.
4. *Faith*: I trust in God that God will enable me to leave behind my old way of life and embrace the new way.
5. *Community*: I open myself to the resources and the love of the people of God to assist me in turning around and to help me stay on the right path.

Here, then, is the paradigm for transformation. *Transformation involves insight, repentance, confession, faith, and community.* In the weeks ahead we will discuss each of these aspects of transformation.

DISCUSSION 10–15 MINUTES

4. Which (if any) of the following types of sudden transformation have you experienced? Describe one such experience as well as the nature of the transformation that took place in your life:

   - ❑ a conversion experience
   - ❑ a mystical experience
   - ❑ a charismatic experience
   - ❑ a prayer experience
   - ❑ a moral transformation
   - ❑ a relational transformation
   - ❑ a career transformation
   - ❑ other: _____

5. If you could pick one area of your life to be transformed suddenly, which might it be? Why?

   - ❑ behavior
   - ❑ lifestyle
   - ❑ thoughts
   - ❑ feelings
   - ❑ relationships
   - ❑ ministry
   - ❑ other _____

6. How does change usually take place in your life?

   - ❑ Suddenly: It takes God's grace to move me
   - ❑ Traumatically: I get hit over the head with something and I change
   - ❑ Slowly: I work on things and gradually it gets better
   - ❑ Invisibly: My friends tell me that something has changed in me

Spiritual Transformation

- ☐ Periodically: Everyone once in a while I work on stuff
- ☐ Gently: A problem will dawn on me and I make changes
- ☐ Incompletely: My life is too disordered for organized change
- ☐ Relationally: I get help from others
- ☐ Internally: I process my life through prayer and reflection
- ☐ Intentionally: I work at change all the time
- ☐ Involuntarily: I don't like change so I resist
- ☐ Humorously: I see how funny (ridiculous) I am being and then I change
- ☐ other: _____

7. Discuss the three descriptions of transformation found above in Mark 1:17, Romans 12:2, and Ephesians 4:22–24:

   - In what ways does following Jesus change a person? What kinds of change have taken place in your life since you have been following Jesus (if you are)?
   - How does "renewing our minds" bring about change in us? What is the connection between how we think and how we live?
   - What do you know about the tension between your "old self" (with its desires) and your "new self" (with its longings)?

APPLICATION 10–15 MINUTES

8. What would men and women be like in their thoughts, feelings, and behaviors if they were fully conformed to the image of Christ?

9. What difference does it make on a day-by-day basis that Christ is in you? How can a person access "the mind of Christ" in ways that make a difference?

10. Read over the following case study taken from everyday life. The problem is not a huge one, but it is real, has spiritual consequences, and illustrates the process of change. Discuss how this case illustrates the five-point outline above of the process of change: insight, repentance, confession, faith, and community.

> My problem is food. I love it. I can't say "No" to it. Needless to say, my weight has become a problem. It is not that I haven't tried a variety of diets. It is just that they do not bring about long-term results. I lose weight for a while but then it creeps back up. However, something new has happened to me. Six months ago I lost 25 pounds and I am keeping that weight off. I now have a whole new way of thinking and acting. Here is what happened.
>
> It all began when I finally got serious about my weight. It was not so much how I looked that bothered me as how I felt. I felt bad and my doctor said that I was not going to feel any better unless I stripped off some weight. His words plus St. Paul's words finally got through to me. (I kept being reminded that the apostle considered our bodies as temples of the Holy Spirit that we were not supposed to mistreat.) I woke up one day and said, "This is it. The weight has got to go." I knew from experience that this decision would have as much weight (pardon the pun) as a New Year's resolution unless I got help. So I did a couple of things.
>
> First, I told everybody about my decision to lose weight. I made my decision public. Now that my friends knew that I was trying to lose weight, they became a team that held me accountable to do what I had proposed. Always in the past I wanted my weight loss to come as a "surprise" to everybody. Also, I guess, I didn't want them on my case if it didn't work out.
>
> Then second, I joined a health club. I knew exercise was one key to weight loss but I never lasted long on any exercise program that I started. Being the creature of habit that I am, I knew that I would have a better chance of success if I signed up for certain exercise slots each week. Besides I'm "tight with money" (as my

friends tell me) and if I paid out good money to a health club, I was not going to waste it.

Third, I started reading about food. I could have joined one of those weight-watcher groups but I learn best by reading. I started getting educated about food and patterns of eating. (Actually, I later learned just how helpful the weight-watcher community could be when it came to losing the pounds.)

It wasn't easy. Some mornings the last thing I wanted to do was go to the gym but by this time I had a partner and he would be picking me up so I had better be ready. Nor was it easy to grasp the complexity of food. It took a long time to get straight where the bad fat and calories were located and how to avoid the worst culprits without eating endlessly tasteless stuff. Actually it turned out to be simple. Eat only real food. Stay away from processed food. Watch calories.

The most important discovery had to do with how I ate. I mean, like that is a big discovery but quite frankly, I had not noticed my patterns. I had not realized that I ate large helpings of food, that I almost always took seconds, that I ate rapidly (I was usually the first one finished at the table), and that I munched on snacks. Another big discovery was what I ate. For a couple of weeks I wrote down in a book every morsel I put in my mouth and every drop I drank. Looking over my entries it became clear that I didn't need all that stuff and that I was eating the wrong stuff. So I changed some patterns. I started putting moderate helpings on my plate (aided by my ever vigilant team of encouragers). I ate only one helping. And I never, never ate between meals (well, almost never). And my food choice was better due to all that reading I had done. (I miss *Ben & Jerry's* ice cream something fierce. However, in terms of full disclosure: I do eat it occasionally, as a special treat.) One of the hardest things was to slow down when I ate. I made it into a game. Could I finish at the same time as one of the slow eaters? Could I actually finish last? Amazingly, the result was that as I paid attention I started tasting the food in a new way.

I had help, of course: my friends, my books, my prayer group, and my own fear that my weight was doing me in physically. But I did it. I lost the target weight and I have kept it off. I suppose my biggest discovery was that what I was involved in was not just a new diet but also a new way of life. It feels good to be walking on the path to a healthier life style.

THE PROCESS OF TRANSFORMATION

PRAYER   5–10 MINUTES

End this small group session with a time of prayer in which you ask God for:

- a deep openness to transformation
- a hunger to become ever more conformed to the image of Christ
- an energized will to make transformation a part of your lifestyle
- an awareness of your need for transformation (a clear sense of how sin in all its forms mars your life)
- a receptive spirit so as to be willing to change those areas of life that do not conform to the will of God.

REFLECTION   During the week

11. Keep musing on the question, "If you could pick one area of your life to be transformed suddenly, which might it be? Why?" Record your reflections in a journal.
12. Reflect on the ways you have changed since you started trying to follow the way of Jesus. Record these reflections in your journal.

Session Two

The Renewing of Our Minds

A Bible Study on Romans 12:1–2

OVERVIEW

In Romans 12 and 13 we find a blueprint for how we are meant to live as followers of Jesus. In very specific, practical terms St. Paul defines for us the goal of transformation. Here he describes the nature of the transformed life. This is what life looks like when it is lived in conformity with the will of God. In this session we begin our six-part study of Romans 12 and 13 by examining the key to transformation: the renewing of our minds. The dynamics of spiritual transformation are defined for us in this passage.

Unison Prayer

Once again begin with a prayer of St. Anselm (1033–1109).

> *O Lord our God, grant us grace to desire you with our whole heart,*
>   *that so desiring, we may seek and find you;*
>   *and so finding you we may love you;*
>   *and loving you we may hate those sins from which you have redeemed us;*
> *for the sake of Jesus Christ. Amen.*[1]

---

1. Ibid., 68.

OPEN   20–30 MINUTES

Small Group Process

A small groups functions best when everyone has a clear sense of how it operates. This is the role of a small group covenant: to define the ground rules for the group. Below you will find a suggested set of guidelines. Examine these together using the questions that follow:

1. Are there any guidelines that you think need to be deleted or altered?

2. Are there other guidelines that you think might profitably be added?

3. What is one hope you have for this small group? What would you like to see happen in it?

4. Are you happy to abide by the agreed upon guidelines for the duration of this small group?

A Small Group Covenant

- *Attendance*: I agree to be at each session unless a genuine emergency arises
- *Preparation*: I will read over the materials, as I am able, in preparation for each small group session.
- *Participation*: I will enter enthusiastically into the group discussion and sharing. I will work on my particular issue of growth and share my experience with the others as appropriate.
- *Intentionality*: I will give my full attention to the group during the session. I will turn-off my cell phone and other devices that might interrupt the group.

- *Prayer*: I will pray for the members of my small group and for our experience together.
- *Confidentiality*: I will not share with anyone outside the group what is said during the group session.
- *Honesty*: I will be forthright and truthful in what I say.
- *Openness*: I will be candid with the others in appropriate ways and I will allow others the freedom to be open in ways appropriate to them.
- *Respect*: I will not judge others, give advice, or criticize.
- *Care*: I will be open to the needs of each other in appropriate ways.

Signed: _____   Date: _____

THE PASSAGE   5 MINUTES

In the two introductory verses that you are going to study in this session (Rom 12:1–2), Paul defines the essence of transformation. Even though you will be examining only two verses, you will find a lot of data and insight packed into these two verses. Romans 12:1–2 shows us how transformation occurs. In the rest of Romans 12 and 13 Paul gives us the specifics of what transformation looks like.

Begin by reading aloud the two renderings of Roman 12:1–2. The *New Revised Standard Version* (NRSV) is a literal translation from the Greek and will be the text that you study together. *The Message* (translated by Eugene Peterson) is a modern day paraphrase of the same passage, which will help you understand the meaning and application of the passage.

Romans 12: 1–2

1I appeal to you therefore, brothers and sisters, by the mercies of God, to present your bodies as a living sacrifice, holy and acceptable to God, which is your spiritual worship. 2Do not be conformed to this world, but be transformed by the renewing of your minds, so that you may discern what is the will of God—what is good and acceptable and perfect. (NRSV)

So here's what I want you to do, God helping you: Take your everyday, ordinary life—your sleeping, eating, going-to-work, and walking-around life—and place it before God as an offering. Embracing what God does for you is the best thing you can do for him. Don't become so well-adjusted to your culture that you fit into it without even thinking. Instead, fix your attention on God. You'll be changed from the inside out. Readily recognize what he wants from you, and quickly respond to it. Unlike the culture around you, always dragging you down to its level of immaturity, God brings the best out of you, develops well-formed maturity in you. (The Message)

ANALYSIS   15–20 MINUTES

In your analysis of these verses, focus on the more literal translation given in the *New Revised Standard Version*. Use *The Message* to shed light on the meaning of the verses.

5. What are the three "commands" (imperatives) or "appeals" Paul gives us?

    - Verse 1 _____
    - Verse 2a _____
    - Verse 2b _____

6. What does each of these commands mean and how can we follow them in our daily lives? How does *The Message* translate each command?

7. What is the outcome when a person does as Paul urges us?

8. What is the transforming process according to these verses?

APPLICATION 15–20 MINUTES

9. What does it mean to you to offer yourself to God? In what ways is this reasonable or rational?

10. What is the message we get from film, television, and radio concerning the following items:

    - money
    - relationships
    - spirituality

11. In what ways are these cultural messages in accord with or in opposition to a biblical perspective ("the will of God")?

12. Here is a paraphrase of the central point of this passage:

    As we think about transformation, the choice is between the pattern of this world and God's will. These two phrases define the two poles toward which we can move in life. Will we continue to walk in the ways of the world or will we stop, turn around, and start following the ways of God? It is this decision that stands at the heart of the transforming process and this decision that we must make over and over again throughout the course of our lives.

    Discuss this paraphrase:

    - To your mind, does this adequately sum up what Paul says in these verses? Why or why not?
    - What practical difference does this way of thinking and acting make for how we live our daily lives?

13. Where are you in your own growth when it comes to the goals identified here, specifically:

    - offering your bodies to God as a living sacrifice?
    - not conforming to the pattern of this world?
    - being transformed by the renewing of your mind?
    - End by reading aloud again *The Message* paraphrase of this passage.

PRAYER   5–15 MINUTES

After each Bible study you will end with a meditative prayer exercise. The aim of this exercise is to open yourself to the guidance God has for you from this passage. The way this exercise works is described in the *Leader's Notes for this Study* at the end of the book.

In this prayer time, reflect on Romans 12:2a. With your eyes closed and minds focused on God, listen as your leader reads aloud, twice, the passage below. As he or she reads, listen for the words or phrase from this selection that resonates with you. In the silence that follows, meditate on those words or phrase. What is God saying to you? How do these words or phrase connect with your life? When the silent meditation ends, join in prayer together offering back to God what you have been thinking and feeling in your meditation.

> *Do not conform any longer to the pattern of this world, but be transformed by the renewing of your mind.*

REFLECTION   During the week

15. Reflect on the unhealthy ways in which you might be "conformed to this world."

16. In what ways does your mind need to be transformed?

17. In your journal, name these ways of conformity to culture that are not leading you in ways that bring wholeness. Reflect on how you might promote the transformation of your mind.

BIBLE STUDY NOTES

Overview

In the first eleven chapters of his letter to the church at Rome, Paul offers a masterful reflection on the great themes that define the essence of the Christian message: sin, salvation, death, resurrection, grace, faith, righteousness, justification, sanctification, and redemption. But his focus shifts in chapter 12. Now he turns his attention from doctrine to duty, from exposition to exhortation, from theory to practical matters. Paul makes this same shift in other letters (e.g., Ephesians). It seems that he is never content simply to offer ideas to his readers. He wants these ideas (about which he cares passionately) to be lived out in everyday life. In his view, Christian ethics emerges out of Christian theology; Christian obedience is a response to Christian truth. So in Romans 12:1–15:13 he brings to a close his great exposition on the work of God in the world by exhorting his readers to live out what they believe. In Romans 12 and 13 Paul describes what life looks like when it is lived in accord with God's will.

Verse 1

Context

This section begins with the phrase, "*I appeal to you therefore.*" The word *therefore* connects what Paul wants to say in this new section (12:1–15:13) with what he has already said up to this point in his letter (chapters 1–11). His comments on what the Christian lifestyle looks like flow directly from what he has said about the work of God on this planet. Christian life flows directly from Christian doctrine. Ideas beget lifestyle. When Paul says, "*I appeal to you,*" it is with the full weight of his apostolic authority. He knows the way to life and health. Paul goes on to name the recipients of the appeal that he is to make: it is *brothers and sisters*, i.e., all believers regardless of their ethnic origin. There have been tensions between the Jews and the non-Jews (Gentiles) in the Roman church, but Paul has argued persuasively in this letter that these ethnic distinctions no longer matter in the church of Jesus Christ.

What Paul first urges us to do is to offer our *bodies* as *living sacrifices*. Of course, he is not referring to our skin and bones but to the totality of our being (as Calvin points out). He uses the word "*bodies*" because he has in mind the Old Testament sacrificial system in which animals were offered to God—their carcasses (bodies) placed on the altar to become the property of God. The three qualifiers attached to the word *sacrifice* are instructive. They are *living*, *holy*, and *acceptable*. This is the kind of sacrifice God wants: one that involves our actions, one that is set apart for God, and one that is in conformity to God's will. Paul does not just urge us to become living sacrifices. He gives us a reason for doing so—*the mercy of God*. Our motivation to obedience is overwhelming gratitude for the many and varied manifestations of God's mercy extended toward us. In the previous eleven chapters Paul has demonstrated the fact of God's mercy.

This dedication of our bodies to God is an act of "*spiritual worship*." The word translated "spiritual" is *logikos*. It can also be translated as "reasonable" or "rational." If it means "reasonable" the idea is that "the offering of ourselves to God is seen as the only sensible, logical and appropriate response to him in view of his self-giving mercy."[2] If the correct sense of the word is "rational" then what we are to offer God is intelligent worship (as J. B. Phillips translates this word) as against mere ceremonial worship.

Connection

It is the experience of God's mercy toward us that is the greatest incentive to living in accord with the way of God. It is when we grasp the many and varied ways in which God extends mercy to us that our gratitude is expressed by living a God-centered life.

At first, it strikes us as odd that God wants our bodies. But worship that is acceptable to him is that which expresses itself in concrete acts of the body. We so often think of worship as inward, mystical, and private. But, in fact, this makes sense when we remember that it is via our bodies that sin expresses itself (as Paul has argued in Rom 3:13–18). It is what we do and say that shows us to be on a path walking away from God. So, when we seek to follow the way of God, that decision is demonstrated in words of healing and acts of mercy. It is what our bodies do that gives evidence as to whom we are following. Transformation is not merely an inner reality; it is seen in our daily actions.

And these acts of worship take place not in the Temple (as with Old Testament worship) but in the home and marketplace. We are called to live out the life of God in whatever circumstances we find ourselves. Worship is not disconnected from life; true worship takes place within the daily ebb and flow of life.

---

2. Stott, *Romans*, 321.

Verse 2

Context

Not only are we to present our *bodies* to God, our *minds* are also to be transformed. This is Paul's second appeal to us. That which binds our minds is *conformity to this world*. This phrase refers to the present evil age (which is passing away) with all of its immorality and corruption. The spirit of this age is set in contrast to *the will of God*.

Do not be conformed is literally, "stop allowing yourself to be conformed," i.e., followers of Jesus are no longer helpless victims of natural and supernatural forces which would shape them into a distorted pattern. Rather they now have the ability to resist such powers and are called upon to resist continuously throughout their life-time (this is the force of the verb tense used here). Likewise, to *be transformed* means to "continue to let yourself be transformed." This is a continuous action by the Holy Spirit that goes on for a lifetime. Our responsibility is to stay open to this process (which, in theological terms, is called sanctification).

The word *transformed* (*metamorphoo*, which is related to the English word *metamorphosis*) is key in understanding what Paul is calling us to. This is the same word that is used in the Gospels to describe the transfiguration of Jesus (Mk 9:2–13). The change in Jesus that the three disciples witnessed on the Mount of Transfiguration was a complete change. The kind of transformation to which we are called is a "fundamental transformation of character and conduct away from the standard of the world and into the image of Christ himself."[3] Such a transformation is brought about by *"the renewing of your minds."* The renewal of our minds involves the development of spiritual sensitivity and perception. We learn to look at life from the point of view of God's understanding of reality. Paul emphasizes the need to develop understanding of God's ways. Paul does not define this process here. However, in other part of the Bible it is clear than such a shift of worldview comes about via the twin work of the Holy Spirit and the Word of God (Scripture). By opening ourselves to the regular study of the Bible with openness to the leading and informing work of the Spirit, how we think begins to shift. We move away from a worldview determined by our culture to a worldview determined by God. Only a renewed mind is capable of doing this. The process of transformation, therefore, begins with renewal of our minds, which gives us the capacity

---

3. Stott, *Romans*, 323.

to discern and desire the will of God, which, in turn, transforms our whole being.

Connection

Paul is calling us to nonconformity. He is urging us not to allow ourselves to be shaped by the world around us. This is not God's way. Rather, we are to be formed by God's will. This is the choice that stands at the heart of the transforming process. Will we simply continue living in accord with the patterns of our culture (which we hardly notice on a conscious level) or will we decide to turn our backs on these ways and follow, instead, God's ways? If we decide to remain in the ways of the world, transformation is not necessary. We will simply go with the flow. But if we chose God's way, this will set us against the currents of our culture. Not completely, not fully because our culture is infused with a sense of God but significantly so in that we will have to say "No" at crucial points. As Barclay has paraphrased this: "Don't be like a chameleon which takes its colour from its surroundings, . . . don't let the world decide what you are going to be like."[4] The verb tense here is instructive. Both the call not to conform and the call to be transformed are present passive imperatives, which means that we are to continue always to resist the world even as we daily open ourselves to be transformed. Nonconformity and transformation are not a one-time decision but a regular and continuing part of our lives as Christians.

---

4. Barclay, *Romans*, 170.

SESSION THREE

Insight

Change Agents that Bring Transformation

OVERVIEW

We cannot even begin the process of change until we become aware of the need for change. In this session we will examine the various ways in which we gain insight into areas that need change.

Unison Prayer

Pray together a prayer from St. Thomas Aquinas (1225–1274) in which he asks for insight and guidance.

> *O creator past all telling, . . .*
> *You we call the true fount of wisdom*
>   *and noble origin of all things.*
> *Be pleased to shed on the darkness of mind in which I was born,*
> *The twofold beam of your light and warmth*
>   *to dispel my ignorance and sin.*
> *You make eloquent the tongues of children.*
> *Then instruct my speech and touch my lips with graciousness.*
> *Make me keen to understand, quick to learn,*
>   *able to remember;*
>   *make me delicate to interpret and ready to speak.*
> *Guide my going in and going forward,*
>   *lead home my going forth.*
> *You are true God and true man,*
>   *and live for ever and ever. Amen*[1]

1. Appleton, *Oxford Book of Prayer*, 92.

SPIRITUAL TRANSFORMATION

OPEN   20–30 MINUTES

"O, now I see what you mean . . ."

It takes a while. Longer for some of us than for others. But eventually we get the point. How are you when it comes to "getting it"?

1. When someone tells a joke, how do you usually respond? (Know any good jokes?)

   - ☐ Is that funny?
   - ☐ I don't get it.
   - ☐ Tell me again so I will remember it.
   - ☐ Not bad, not bad.
   - ☐ That is hilarious.
   - ☐ What?
   - ☐ Why?
   - ☐ What's the point?

2. Where do the insights that make the most sense to you tend to come from? Give an example, if you can.

   - ☐ books
   - ☐ prayer
   - ☐ conversation
   - ☐ film and television
   - ☐ other: _____
   - ☐ sermons
   - ☐ spouse/family
   - ☐ Bible
   - ☐ art/music
   - ☐ parents
   - ☐ meditation
   - ☐ worship
   - ☐ wise elders

3. What do you do with such insights?

   - ☐ reflect on them
   - ☐ write them down in my journal
   - ☐ pray about them
   - ☐ write (paint/sing) about them
   - ☐ use them in a conversation or lecture
   - ☐ other _____
   - ☐ discuss them with others
   - ☐ forget them
   - ☐ put them into practice
   - ☐ neglect them

CONSIDER   15–20 MINUTES

Why change if we don't have to? This seems to be the unconscious logic that guides our lives and keeps us locked into patterns that have outlived their usefulness. I think the core problem is that nobody likes to change. To change is to admit we need to change. It is to admit that we are wrong, inadequate, foolish, unconscious, in denial, or in some other state of being that is less than perfect. Who wants to be wrong? Who wants to admit wrong? So we stick with the way things have always been.

But growth is all about change. You can't grow if you don't change. But without the sense that you *need to change* the whole process is stymied.

Insight is the foundation of transformation.

We need to see the way things really are before we are open to change. Without insight into our own dynamics that need upgrading, we resist, we deny, we protest, we blame, we procrastinate, we refuse to see—denial is the antitheses to insight.

Case in point: Sam is a warm, funny, bright, caring man. People like to be around him—that is, until he gets on one of his hobbyhorses. Sam has strong, dogmatic ideas about a lot of things. Having strong ideas is not the problem. Refusing to see any other point of view is the issue. Sam finds it impossible to admit that there may be another way to think about certain matters.

Clearly Sam needs to step back and listen to others, even if he disagrees with them. He needs to respect the integrity of those who differ with him. But Sam doesn't see the problem. Friends have tried to help him see this character quirk but he just gets mad. Until Sam grasps the problem, until he sees how he impacts others, until he has insight into what he is doing, nothing is going to change. *Denial is the enemy of transformation.*

All this means that it often takes a powerful force to blast us off the status quo and open us up to new options. In this session we are going to explore some of the *agents of change* that bring about new insight into the way things really are with us and thus make it possible for us to grow.

Scripture as Change Agent

When it comes to Christian transformation one of the most potent forces for change is the Bible. The Bible works on us in many different ways. For example, it can be like a *mirror* to us in which we see ourselves for who we truly are. When we read Scripture, we see ourselves reflected back. So, for example, you might read Jesus' words in the Sermon on the Mount, "You have heard that it was said, 'You shall love your neighbor and hate your enemy.' But I say to you, Love your enemies and pray for those who persecute you . . . " (Matt 5:43–44). And in your heart you know that Jesus is speaking to you. You realize that you know about hating enemies ("Yes, I am like that"). But you do not know much about loving enemies and praying for them. So an important truth about yourself is revealed; an attitude that requires change.

At other times Scripture works on us by means of *resonance*. We read a story and discern a connection between the person in the story and ourselves. So, for example, you read the story of Peter when the serving girl confronts him at the time of Jesus' arrest (Matt 26:69–75). She claims that Peter knew Jesus. Peter swears (in both senses of the word!) that this is not the case. As you read this incident, your heart resonates with this experience. You remember a betrayal on your part. The boss asked you about John, your co-worker. You minimized his contribution to the year-end report in order to make your own contribution look better. In fact, John had done as much work as anyone. You are convicted. You know that you will have to deal with this situation both in its immediate ramification (you must go to your boss and tell her the truth; you must go to John and tell him what you did) and in its long-term implications (you must figure out what made you do this and why). Something in you needs to change.

Scripture is also like a *ruler* or *measuring device* especially when it comes to our character. We look into the Bible and see what we should be and then we measure ourselves against this standard. For example, the Bible says, "Speak the truth in love" (Eph. 4:15, NIV). So I ask myself, "Is this how I relate to others?" After I get over my initial declaration that, "Of course this is how I act. I'm a Christian," I start to look deeper. I begin to realize that my tendency is to shade the truth for the sake of love. I do not want to hurt people. Or that is what I tell myself. Maybe the truth is that I fear the disapproval of others and so shy away from the hard edges of truth? Thus the reflection goes on until I get at the heart of the matter. The end result is insight and insight is where change begins.

Scripture brings insight in a variety of ways:

- It *challenges* us to move forward to wholeness by giving us a glimpse of how we should be living.
- It *defines* for us what it means to be living in the image of Christ.

- It *confronts* us by holding up a standard to follow.
- It *confirms* us in behaviors that go against the cultural grain but which are right.
- It *models* for us how to think, act, and feel.
- It *teaches* us about the way things really are, e.g., who God is and how God relates to us.
- It *clarifies* our decisions.
- It *speaks* directly to us as the Word of God.

Scripture touches on a host of areas by way of insight:

- *World view*: It corrects our perceptions of the world. It helps us see things through the lens of the supernatural rather than through the conventional wisdom of our culture.
- *Moral values*: It gives us the basis on which to make decisions when it comes to how we treat others. In fact, it contains the core principles that guide how we make choices in life.
- *Relationships with others*: It defines for us in great detail the path of love.
- *Behavior and Lifestyle*: It describes the actions and attitudes that bring life.
- *Attitudes*: It models for us how to respond to the situations of life.

The Community as a Change Agent

The Christian community is also a source of insight into what we should be become and how we need to change. In fact, this is what the Christian community is all about: growth together in the ways of God.

Our community brings insight in various ways:

- *Worship*: Times of worship are a great stimulus to growth. Via the prayers (which ask for change, amongst other things), in the sermons (that hold up biblical goals for us), and through the readings (that challenge us to conform to the way of God) we gain enormous insight.
- *Fellowship*: It is the love of others that brings insight into who we are.

- *Godly Insight*: There are wise men and women in the church to whom we should listen in order to know ourselves.
- *Small Groups*: In a safe environment in which everyone is seeking to know God's way, insights into ourselves are allowed to surface.
- *Spiritual Experiences*: At times God confronts us directly with the way things really are.

The Gospel as a Change Agent

The gospel of Jesus Christ is all about change—the most radical and comprehensive change of all. The good news (or gospel) is that because of Christ's death and resurrection we can come back to God. We can reclaim our birthright as children of God. It is not that God ever left us. We left God by the choices we made. But Jesus died for our sins ("sin" is the name for our choices against God). Because he died we can be forgiven. We claim this forgiveness by turning to Christ in repentance and faith (more about these two movements in later sessions). In so doing we come in touch with the supernatural side of life. We cease living solely in the world of sense and time and begin living, as well, in the world of spirit. This brings about an enormous change in our lives. In fact, spiritual transformation begins (in some senses) at this point. We are opened up to the spiritual. We begin to move actively in that realm. It is not that we leave behind or deny the wonderful world of sight and sound that God has created for us. Rather, our experience is enriched and broadened; it is made more comprehensive.

So, a clear apprehension of who Jesus is and what his death and resurrection mean to you is the primary insight that begets spiritual transformation.

Other Transforming Agents

Other transforming agents can be named. Such things as books, music, family, dreams, counselors, crises, and the media all have the power to spark new insight into the way things really are for us. In fact, one might even say that all of life is full of the kind of input that reveals truth—if we have eyes to see, ears to hear, and the will to understand. In the end, it does not matter so much from what source the insight arises as long as it has the stamp of God's truth upon it. We know that this is of God when the insight is in alignment with Scripture and Christian tradition, when it promotes our turning toward God, and when those who know us best as spiritual friends and counselors affirm the correctness of the insight.

The Holy Spirit

We have been discussing the means by which insight comes. But behind each of these means is the Holy Spirit. It is the Holy Spirit who uses these means to our spiritual advantage. To talk about spiritual transformation is to talk about the work of the Holy Spirit. How does the Holy Spirit work in our lives to bring about transformation? That is a topic in itself. Suffice it to say that the Spirit works in ways appropriate to who we are and to the end desired by God.

An Attitude of Openness

Of course, none of these change agents will impact us unless we have a heart open to growth. Growth is an attitude as much as anything. It is a kind of divine restlessness that keeps pushing us forward, not allowing us to rest on past accomplishments. We can, of course, mute this inner impulse by simply refusing to pay attention. However, it is hard to do this if one works at the spiritual disciplines. The very process of opening ourselves to God on a regular basis in specific ways keeps us in touch with this inner moving of Spirit of God who desires our wholeness and holiness.

DISCUSSION 10–15 MINUTES

4. Which of the following descriptive phrases best defines how the Bible connects with you? Give examples if you can.

   ☐ It is mirror in which I see myself. ☐ It challenges me.

   ☐ It resonates with my story. ☐ It defines my goals.

   ☐ It is my standard to follow. ☐ It confronts me.

   ☐ It confirms me. ☐ It clarifies my decisions.

   ☐ It models for me how to think and act.

   ☐ It speaks directly to me.

   ☐ It teaches me about the way things really are.

5. Which aspect of your life in the Christian community most stimulates you to growth? Give examples if you can.

   ☐ Worship ☐ Fellowship ☐ Godly Insight

   ☐ Spiritual Experiences ☐ Small Groups

   ☐ Other _____

6. What other agents of insight impact you? Give examples.

   ☐ books ☐ music ☐ family

   ☐ dreams ☐ counselors ☐ crises

   ☐ media/arts

APPLICATION 10–15 MINUTES

7. Do you find new insight into yourself a desirable experience, a troubling experience, or a mixture of the two? Explain your answer.

8. When, if ever, did the good news about Jesus become good news for you personally? What change did commitment to Jesus make in your life?

9. In the days ahead, what are practical things you can do to be open and alert to transforming insight?

    - ❏ Keep a journal
    - ❏ Pray and be open to change
    - ❏ Meet with others who want to grow
    - ❏ Seek spiritual counseling
    - ❏ Open yourself to Scripture
    - ❏ Discuss the direction of your life with those closest to you
    - ❏ Other _____

PRAYER 5–10 MINUTES

End this small group session with a time of prayer in which you ask God for:

- openness to insight into the ways things really are
- the ability to take in and comprehend new insights
- the willingness to open yourself to the transforming power of the Bible, Church, and other vehicles
- awareness of areas in which growth is needed

REFLECTION During the week

10. Name one area in your life that you know needs changing. Perhaps it has to do with a relationship or with conduct at work or with behaviors that do not lead to wholeness or with fears that paralyze you, or (you name the issue).

11. In your journal, reflect on this issue: what it is, how it manifests itself, what its causes might be, who it impacts, etc. Describe the history this behavior.

SESSION FOUR

Knowing Ourselves

A Bible Study on Romans 12:3–8

OVERVIEW

Transformation begins with a "sober" view of ourselves, so Paul teaches us. We need to know who we are, what we wrestle with, how we function in our day-by-day life, and what is going on below the surface of our lives. Such knowledge is not easy to come by. For example, we tend to overestimate (or underestimate) our skills, abilities, and accomplishments. So maybe the place to begin this "sober judgment" is with the particular spiritual gifts we have been given, as Paul suggests. We all have gifts. We need to be able to name these so we can use our gifts in the context of the Christian community of which we are part. Once we see our strengths, then it becomes easier to name our weaknesses. We all have weaknesses. Our weaknesses (shortcomings) are exactly what need to be transformed.

Unison Prayer

Begin with a prayer by George Appleton, the editor of *The Oxford Book of Prayer*, in which you invite the Holy Spirit into your pursuit of wholeness.

> *O Holy Spirit, whose presence is liberty, grant us that freedom of the spirit, which will not fear to tread in unknown ways, nor be held back by misgivings of ourselves and fear of others. Even beckon us forward to the place of your will which is also the place of your power, O ever-leading, ever-loving Lord. Amen.*[1]

---

1. Ibid., 148.

SPIRITUAL TRANSFORMATION

OPEN   20–30 MINUTES

The Things You Do Best

We all have talents. We all have special skills. But sometimes it takes us a while to recognize these. What are you good at?

1. When you were a kid, in what activity did you shine?

   - ❐ drawing
   - ❐ singing
   - ❐ playing
   - ❐ competing
   - ❐ reading
   - ❐ hanging out
   - ❐ watching TV
   - ❐ winning games
   - ❐ everything
   - ❐ nothing
   - ❐ other _____

2. When you were in high school, what was you favorite subject? How have you used this interest and ability in later life?

   - ❐ math
   - ❐ literature
   - ❐ science
   - ❐ history
   - ❐ gym
   - ❐ social studies
   - ❐ driver's education
   - ❐ skipping school
   - ❐ other _____

3. If you had to name one accomplishment of which you are proud, what would it be?

THE PASSAGE   5 MINUTES

Read aloud the following passage, first in the one translation and then in the other.

Romans 12:3–8

3For by the grace given to me I say to everyone among you not to think of yourself more highly than you ought to think, but to think with sober judgment, each according to the measure of faith that God has assigned. 4For as in one body we have many members, and not all the members have the same function, 5so we, who are many, are one body in Christ, and individually we are members one of another. 6We have gifts that differ according to the grace given to us: prophecy, in proportion to faith; 7ministry, in ministering; the teacher, in teaching;

8the exhorter, in exhortation; the giver, in generosity; the leader, in diligence; the compassionate, in cheerfulness. (NRSV)

I'm speaking to you out of deep gratitude for all that God has given me, and especially as I have responsibilities in relation to you. Living then, as every one of you does, in pure grace, it's important that you not misinterpret yourselves as people who are bringing this goodness to God. No, God brings it all to you. The only accurate way to understand ourselves is by what God is and by what he does for us, not by what we are and what we do for him.

In this way we are like the various parts of a human body. Each part gets its meaning from the body as a whole, not the other way around. The body we're talking about is Christ's body of a chosen people. Each of us finds our meaning and function as a part of his body. But as a chopped-off finger or cut-off toe we wouldn't amount to much, would we? So since we find ourselves fashioned into all these excellently formed and marvelously functioning parts in Christ's body, let's just go ahead and be what we were made to be, without enviously or pridefully comparing ourselves with each other, or trying to be something we aren't.

If you preach, just preach God's Message, nothing else; if you help, just help, don't take over; if you teach, stick to your teaching; if you give encouraging guidance, be careful that you don't get bossy; if you're put in charge, don't manipulate; if you're called to give aid to people in distress, keep your eyes open and be quick to respond; if you work with the disadvantaged, don't let yourself get irritated with them or depressed by them. Keep a smile on your face. (The Message)

ANALYSIS   15–20 MINUTES

4. What is the correct attitude that we should have about ourselves and about our gifts, according to Paul? What is the basis for such an attitude?

5. What is the point of Paul's word-picture in verses 4–5 and what is he trying to teach us?

SPIRITUAL TRANSFORMATION

6. List the seven gifts identified in this passage. Discuss what each gift involves, illustrating this by reference to your experience of people who have this particular gift, including your own experience of this gift.

   1.
   2.
   3.
   4.
   5.
   6.
   7.

7. What does this section from Romans contribute to your understanding of the nature of the Christian life?

APPLICATION   15–20 MINUTES

8. Which is easier for you: to have too high a view of yourself or to have too low a view of yourself? Why?

9. Peter Wagner says that discerning one's spiritual gift is a five-part process:
   - *Explore* the whole idea of spiritual gifts in Scripture, in your church, and in other literature. You want to know as much as you can about spiritual gifts.
   - *Experiment* with as many gifts as possible. In this way you will learn what gifts you do not have as well as begin to know what gift(s) you do have.
   - *Examine* your feelings. You will enjoy exercising your gift.
   - *Evaluate* your effectiveness. If it really is your gift, you will experience success in its use.

- *Seek confirmation* from the Christian body of which you are a part that they do, indeed, believe you to be so gifted.[2]

Discuss Wagner's proposal. What have you discovered as you have sought to identify your spiritual gift(s)? Or, what is the next step for you in identifying your own gift?

10. Gifts do not come to us full-blown. A person may have the gift of teaching, for example, but she needs study and training in order to become a gifted teacher in the church. Where are you in your own gift-education?

11. Ministry is an issue of transformation. All of us are all called to ministry of one sort or another using the gift(s) God has given us. That ministry may be in the context of the local church. It may focus on the home. It may find expression in the marketplace or neighborhood. But we all have a ministry. The challenge is finding our gift, growing in it, and using it.

    - How would you describe your role in the body of Christ? Where do you fit? What do you contribute? What is your spiritual gift(s)?
    - What is your ministry or how can you discern your ministry?

12. Where are you in your own growth when it comes to the goals identified in this passage:

    - having an accurate view of yourself?
    - understanding the nature of the Christian community?
    - knowing clearly the gifts you have been given by God for use in that community?

13. End this section by reading aloud again *The Message* paraphrase of this passage.

---

2. Wagner, *Your Spiritual Gifts Can Help Your Church Grow*, 116-133.

PRAYER 5–15 MINUTES

In your prayer together, focus on the following selection from Romans 12:5–6a. With your eyes closed and minds focused on God, listen as your leader reads aloud the passage below twice. As he or she reads, listen for the words or phrase from this selection that resonates with you. In the silence that follows, meditate on those words or phrase. What is God saying to you? How do these words or phrase connect with your life? When the silent meditation ends, join in prayer together offering back to God what you have been thinking and feeling in your meditation.

> *So we, who are many, are one body in Christ, and individually we are members one of another. We have gifts that differ . . .*

End by praying for the person on your right, asking for God's guidance and blessing on his/her ministry.

REFLECTION During the week

14. What is your spiritual gift? How do you know? How do you use this gift? What can you do by way of training to enhance this gift? Reflect on this issue of spiritual gifts.

15. Do you think more highly of yourself than you ought? Reflect on this in your journal. Do a "sober assessment" of yourself.

BIBLE STUDY NOTES
Overview

Paul has called us to a renewed mind in verses 1–2. Such a mind is capable of both discerning (testing) and approving the will of God. In verses 3–8 he invites us to turn our minds to the question of who we actually are (note the repetition of "think" in verse 3). It is important that we have a clear and accurate sense of ourselves as we seek to live out, in reality, a transformed lifestyle. There are three concerns in this section: that we have an accurate view of ourselves, that we understand the nature of the Christian community, and that we know clearly the gifts that we have been given by God for use in that community.

Verse 3

Context

Paul begins by addressing each and every member of the church in Rome ("everyone among you"). No one is excluded. All need to have the same humble self-assessment ("think with sober judgment") and all have been given spiritual gifts ("we have gifts that differ"). He addresses them as an apostle (which is probably what he means when he says "by the grace given to me"). His call to *sober judgment* is a call to know oneself accurately (especially one's gifts) rather than to have too high an opinion of oneself in comparison to others (as this verse might be interpreted). This attitude enables a community of believers to blend their gifts together in harmonious ministry. He goes on to say that Christians are not to measure themselves against others but against the standard God has given them in their faith. Since these gifts come from God there is no basis for superiority on the part of anyone.

Connection

It is hard to see ourselves as we truly are but this is our calling from God. In the previous session we discussed various inputs that bring insight. We focused on areas in our lives that need change, i.e., areas in which we have not yet got it right. But in this passage the focus is the other way around: on areas in which we have got it right. Quite frankly, it is harder for many people to claim their strengths than it is for them to name their weaknesses. Part of this is cultural. We are taught not to brag or be too self-important. Another part of this is that we simply take for granted what we do best. We assume everybody does it well. So we do not notice our own talents. But in not noticing our talents we can't thank God for them or use them consciously for God's glory. Knowing ourselves is an important matter in our growth. *Self-knowledge is the foundation on which transformation is built.*

Verses 4 & 5

Context

Paul uses the image of a body in order to explain the nature of the Christian community. Just as the human body has different parts (hands, feet, eyes, legs, hair, etc.) so too the Christian community is made up of various people, each of whom has a different gift or function (teaching, leading, encouraging, etc.). Interestingly, this is a word picture (the body) that can be understood in every culture and needs little translation. Paul also asserts that "we are members of one another." This is a remarkable statement in light of the tension between Jews and Gentiles in the Roman church. Paul's point is that there is a unity that binds all together and it is with that reality in mind that we need to see our differences. Paul also describes the basis of this unity: we are all "in Christ." It is that fact which makes this unity possible. This is spiritual unity.

Connection

If we really understood and acted upon the image Paul gives us of the church, our problems with one another would be greatly lessened. We are all part of one another—members of a great, worldwide community made up of those who seek to follow Jesus. We have no choice in the matter. In following Jesus we become part of this community. But in the midst of this essential unity (what a great gift it is), there is also great diversity. We all have a part to play in the healthy functioning of the body. (Remember verse 3, no one is exempted). But we have different roles to play. Part of our sober assessment of ourselves has to do with understanding what gift we have and then using it for the sake of others.

Verse 6

Context

By way of illustration Paul now describes seven representative gifts. Three gifts have to do with speaking; four have to do with service. The Greek word for "gifts" is *charismata* and is closely related to the Greek word for "grace" (*charis*). These are grace-gifts, intended to be used in the service of others. The list of gifts here (and in 1 Cor 12 and in Eph 4:11–12) is not meant to be exhaustive or complete since no gift-list overlaps fully. Instead, they are illustrative of what spiritual gifts are like. There are other spiritual gifts that have not been named in these lists. The first gift mentioned is *prophesying* which is a kind of speaking under divine inspiration. Inspired utterances are distinguished from teaching by their immediacy and unpremeditated nature, the source of which is direct revelation by God. They are often directed to concrete situations and at times have to do with the future (Acts 11:27–30). At other times prophecy concerns what God wants done (Acts 13:11–12). Both men and women prophesy (Acts 21:9) and they do so in words that are readily understood (as opposed to ecstatic speech known as "tongues"). Prophesying was highly valued in the New Testament church (1 Cor 14:1). The phrase "in proportion to faith" probably means that prophets must make sure their utterances are in accord with the "faith," i.e., Christian doctrine.

Connection

Spiritual gifts are not some sort of inner, ethereal endowment that makes one feel good. They are actual abilities that we are meant to use both within and without the church. It is very important to note that spiritual gifts are never given for one's own sake. Just as Jesus never performed a miracle for his own sake, we too are to use these gifts for others. They are, indeed, "the grace-gifts given for others." Prophesy is the most interesting of the seven gifts listed in that it involves direct contact with the supernatural. It is also one of those gifts that causes people to wonder. Who dares to claim that what he or she speaks is directly from God? Yet the gift of prophecy is named and was widely used in the early church.

Verse 7

Context

Two more gifts are named. The Greek word translated here as *ministry* is *diakonia* (from which the English word diaconate is derived). This word is used to describe a variety of ministries. For example, the ministry of the word of God by the apostles and the ministry of waiting on tables by the seven are both called *diakonia* (see Acts 6:1–4). *Teaching* is familiar to us. In contrast to the prophet whose utterances has as their source the direct revelation of God, the first-century teacher relied on the Old Testament scriptures and the teachings of Jesus to instruct others.

Connection

These two gifts focus on the needs of body and mind. There was never a distinction in the early church between ministry that attended to spiritual or intellectual needs and ministry that focused on physical needs. Both were important. Both were activities of the church.

Verse 8

Context

The final four gifts are named in this verse. The Greek word translated *the exhorter* has a variety of meanings including encouragement, comforting, consoling, and conciliating. The gift of *the giver* has to do with giving away one's possessions for the sake of others. Such generosity needs to be done freely and willingly, without ulterior motives. The gift of *the leader* refers to those who have been given the ability to guide congregations. They are to do so with diligence. Finally the gift of *the compassionate* has to do with those in a congregation who care for others who are in need, be it widows, the aged, orphans, the ill, or the dying. Such compassion (or mercy) must be given cheerfully, without patronization.

Connection

These are not all the gifts listed in the New Testament. Other gifts include: healing, hospitality, evangelism, celibacy, wisdom, faith, knowledge, miracles, discerning of spirits, tongues, the interpretation of tongues, being an apostle, being a pastor-teacher, and being a missionary. A lot of people would argue that there are yet more gifts as well. Some would name the gifts of intercession and exorcism as examples.

SESSION FIVE

Repentance

The Decision to Change

OVERVIEW

It is one thing to see the problem; it is quite another to decide to do something about it. In fact, even when we know that certain patterns of behavior, ways of thinking, or processes of feeling are counter-productive, we do not act to change our life. This is where repentance comes into the picture. Repentance is the theological word for *the decision to change*. It is a vital step in the transformation process. In this session we will explore the meaning of repentance and its practical application in a life of transformation.

Unison Prayer

Pray together a prayer of repentance from Eric Milner-White (1884–1964).

> *O God our Father, help us to nail to the cross of your dear Son the whole body of our death, the wrong desires of the heart, the sinful devisings of the mind, the corrupt apprehensions of the eyes, the cruel words of the tongue, the ill employment of hands and feet; that the old man being crucified and done away, the new man may live and grow into the glorious likeness of the same your Son Jesus Christ, who lives and reigns with you and the Holy Ghost, one God, world without end. Amen.*[1]

---

1. Appleton, *Oxford Book of Prayer*, 107.

SPIRITUAL TRANSFORMATION

OPEN   20–30 MINUTES
Indiscretions

Nobody can avoid them. We all have "momentary lapses" and "embarrassing moments." How do you handle your behavior when it is less than perfect?

1. When you were a kid, what was one really naughty thing you did? What happened as a result?

2. What sort of "explanation" did you give when you got caught (or were suspected)?

   ☐ "My brother (sister) made me do it."

   ☐ "Problem, what problem?"

   ☐ "I can't imagine how that happened?"

   ☐ "Well, it all started when I was 3 years old . . . " (and a long story unfolds)

   ☐ "Don't blame me."

   ☐ "The dog/cat/gerbil ate it."

   ☐ "You can't think I'd do a thing like that!"

   ☐ "I plead the Fifth."

   ☐ "I'm sure there is a rational explanation for all this."

   ☐ "Why worry over little things."

   ☐ "If it makes you feel better, I'm sorry."

3. As a teen-ager, what was one "embarrassing moment" which was actually your fault?

CONSIDER   15–20 MINUTES
The Experience of Transformation

What do we do with insight? Insight alone does not produce change. In fact, insight, by itself, cannot bring change. Insight is just that: awareness that something is so. There is no inherent dynamic connected to insight.

This is why there is a second step in the process of transformation. The response to insight that launches change is something called "repentance."

The Definition of Repentance

Repentance is not a word we use regularly. It has a slightly archaic sound to it; like something out of the medieval church or perhaps from the tents of revivalists with their sawdust trails. It conjures up images of white-robed men carrying signs saying, "Repent, the world is coming to an end." But, in fact, repentance is quite a respectable biblical word. It is used literally thousands of times in the Old Testament (usually in reference to the people of Israel) and scores of times in the New Testament.

Repentance simply means, "to change your mind." It is that straightforward. The context of that change has to do with God. To repent is to change your mind about how you are living in relationship to God. It is to understand (insight) that all is not well; that you are, in fact not walking in God's way. It is to decide (repentance) to change that state of affairs by turning around and going God's way.

Even though repentance is not a normal part of our vocabularies we do understand it in one context. We know it has to do with conversion. We understand that repentance is all about the decision to stop following the ways of the world and to start following Jesus Christ. It has to do with our decision to go God's way. But what we often fail to realize is that repentance is not just a one-time action. To grow in the Christian life we must go on repenting—as we continue to discover issues about which we have got it wrong.

And we do get it wrong in a lot of different areas:

- *How we think*: The fact of the matter is that even with the best will in the world and even with a bright mind and a good education we will never understand everything accurately. As human beings there are limits to our knowledge and to our ability to comprehend. This also applies to understanding the ways of God. No matter how good a Bible student you might be, your knowledge will always be partial. Knowing this should make us open to explore truth and willing to change our minds when we discover we have been wrong. The Christian life is a pilgrimage of the mind as much as anything else. To repent in the cognitive area of life is to say, "I misunderstood. I got it wrong" and then move beyond our inadequate understanding.

- *How we feel*: Feelings are notoriously difficult for some people to get at. And yet it is how we feel that gives energy and meaning to life. When we move into the realm of feeling it is not so much a matter of proper vs. improper feelings. Feelings are feelings. They come. We have little control over them. We are mad, sad, glad, or fearful. The issue is not what we feel but what we do with our feelings. For example, Paul says "Be angry, but do not sin; do not let the sun go down on your anger" (Eph 4:26, quoting Ps 4:4). We get angry, all of us, no exceptions. Anger is not the problem (or the sin). Paul says we have to deal with our anger least it turn into sin by behaving badly. Growth comes as we learn how to deal with our emotions in healthy ways. To repent in the affective area of life is to say, "I did not handle that feeling very well" and aim at doing better the next time such feelings surface.

- *How we behave*: We all have a lot of room to grow when it comes to our behavior and lifestyle. How we live and what we do seems to be shaped more by our culture (and what is acceptable vs. unacceptable) than by our faith. This is why there is the strange disjunction in many of our lives between the ethic of the Bible (to which we are supposedly committed) and the ethic of the marketplace (by which we actually function on a daily basis). To repent in the behavioral area of life is to say, "I did not do that right" and then starting to do it right as much as is possible.

- *How we relate*: Love is the central command by which we are meant to live and yet it is safe to say that in all of our lives it is in the realm of personal relationships that we have the greatest difficulty and where the greatest growth needs to take place. Relationships are endlessly complex and so we need to work on them continuously. To repent in the relational area is to say, "I did not act in a loving way toward that person" and seek to do better in the future.

You see what repentance is at its root? It is recognizing failure and deciding to do something about it. Repentance needs to become a reflexive response and not just an occasional moment of deep regret. Repentance is a friend because it leads to growth, not an enemy because it requires admitting to wrong. Repentance needs to become a familiar and comfortable response in our daily lives.

Sin

It is time to talk about sin. Sin is one of those words we don't like and which we misunderstand. When most people hear the word "sin" what pops into their minds is some sort of gross misdeed like robbing a bank, beating up a person, or committing adultery. In fact, this is an accurate understanding of the word but it is a sadly limited understanding of what sin is all about. By making sin into only really bad actions, we are able to act as if sin is not something we do (except, perhaps, occasionally). But sin is far more domestic than we realize. It also encompasses all the little things we do—the white lies, the small cruelties, and the mundane failures. You see, sin is not just what we do wrong (trespasses); it also how we fail (shortcomings).

The word sin is used frequently in the Bible (as everyone knows). But in Greek and Hebrew "sin" is not a single word as in English. There are various words that are translated by this one English word. However, all these biblical words tend to cluster around two images:

- The image of transgression. To sin is to cross the fence and go into your neighbor's forbidden field, it is to steal that which belongs to another, and it is to go against God's commandment to love others.
- The image of shortcoming. To sin is also like an archer shooting arrows at a target, none of which hit the bulls-eye. They all fall short. To sin, in this sense, is to be unable to live the kind of wholesome life you want to live, it is to fail to understand properly what the Bible is saying to you, and it is not noticing the hungry and dispossessed in our midst.

If we have trouble when it comes to personal identification with sin as trespass (since we really do try to follow God's ways), we have no trouble at all identifying with sin as failure (since we are all too aware that we don't always get it right). The *Book of Common Prayer* speaks of sins of commission (doing evil) and sins of omission (not doing good). Sin is choosing to do the wrong, to embrace evil, and to relish the bad. Sin is also not getting it right, not doing the right, and not understanding what is right.

Sin is what needs to be changed in order to grow. This is what insight is all about: the recognition of our sin. This is what repentance is all about: the decision to deal with our sin. This is what growth is all about: the attempt to move beyond our sin (as best we can).

God and Sin

One more aspect of sin needs to be considered. In the eyes of God, sin is not just an unfortunate lapse or an understandable error. Sin is serious, really serious business. It is sin that creates a barrier between God and us. This is, in part, why Jesus came to our planet: to deal with the problem of sin. This is why he died. His death paid the price for our sin. His death opened up the way for us to go back home to God. There are a lot of theories as to why his death had this effect. But all we really need to know and believe is that, "God proves his love for us in that while we still were sinners, Christ died for us" (Rom 5:8).

One final note: it is the assurance of forgiveness that makes repentance possible and it is the death of Jesus on our behalf that secures our forgiveness. Unless we know that what we see in our lives and name as sin will be forgiven, we will not feel free to explore our lives. But it is because we are assured of forgiveness that we do open ourselves to the insights that reveal the darkness that is in us. Thus the whole growth process can go forward.

DISCUSSION   10–15 MINUTES

4. There are two key words that we need to understand. Discuss together the definition of:

    - repentance
    - sin

5. How does repentance launch the growth process?

6. Why is sin serious business to God and what has God done about the sin problem?

APPLICATION   10–15 MINUTES

You may wish to break up into sub-groups of four in order to allow more time for discussion during this part of the small group. What you will discuss is the crucial question when it comes to transformation. Are you willing to work on your own issues or not? If your answer is yes, then the work of transformation can go forward. If your answer is no, the discussion becomes academic and not personal. By being open about your own struggles you allow the transforming process to move from head to heart. But you must be comfortable with what you share.

7. What are the issues, if any, that you are dealing with at this point in time when it comes to the following areas:

    - What you think/believe?
    - How you handle feelings?
    - How you behave (including lifestyle)?
    - How you relate to others?

PRAYER   5–10 MINUTES

End this small group session with a time of prayer in which you ask God for:

- a clear understanding of both sin and repentance
- an awareness of the power of sin in your life
- the ability to discern those areas that need change
- the will to repent
- the courage to share with others the nature of your struggle in ways that will assist your growth

REFLECTION   During the week

Keep working on the *Application* question:

8. What are the issues, if any, that you are dealing with at this point in time when it comes to the following areas:

    - What you think/believe?
    - How you handle feelings?
    - How you behave (including lifestyle)?
    - How you relate to others?

9. Select one small issue and "repent" of it, i.e., discuss the issue with God. ask for insight, reflect on what you hear, ask for forgiveness if that is appropriate, and then pray a prayer of repentance. Stay aware of how this makes you feel? Think? Behave?

Session Six

Loving Others

A Bible Study on Romans 12:9–16

OVERVIEW

Paul shifts his focus from the diversity of gifts within the Christian body to the quality of relationships that ought to characterize such a community. If there is one word that defines the nature of such relationships (and the whole of the Christian life) it is the word *love*. We need to learn how to love one another within the body of Christ. Then, that way of love becomes the basic pattern by which we relate to all people.

Unison Prayer

Begin with a prayer by St. Anselm (1033–1109) in which we ask for the ability to love others.

> *O blessed Lord, who has commanded us to love one another, grant us grace that having received your undeserved bounty, we may love everyone in you and for you. We implore your clemency for all; but especially for the friends whom your love has given to us. Love them, O fountain of love, and make them to love you with all their heart, that they may will, and speak, and do those things only which are pleasing to you. Amen*[1]

---

1. Ibid., 113.

SPIRITUAL TRANSFORMATION

OPEN   **20–30 MINUTES**

Groups

It is unlikely that you will have grown up in a particular church and remained there your whole life. Most of us move around too much for that to happen. So, you probably have been involved with more than one Christian community—for better or for worse.

1. List quickly all the churches and other Christian groups with which you have been involved.

2. What was your favorite Christian community and why?

3. In your mind, what is the ideal church like?

LOVING OTHERS

THE PASSAGE   **5 MINUTES**

Read aloud the following passage in both translations.

Romans 12:9–16

9Let love be genuine; hate what is evil, hold fast to what is good; 10love one another with mutual affection; outdo one another in showing honor. 11Do not lag in zeal, be ardent in spirit, serve the Lord. 12Rejoice in hope, be patient in suffering, persevere in prayer. 13Contribute to the needs of the saints; extend hospitality to strangers.

14Bless those who persecute you; bless and do not curse them. 15Rejoice with those who rejoice, weep with those who weep. 16Live in harmony with one another; do not be haughty, but associate with the lowly; do not claim to be wiser than you are. (NRSV)

Love from the center of who you are; don't fake it. Run for dear life from evil; hold on for dear life to good. Be good friends who love deeply; practice playing second fiddle.

Don't burn out; keep yourselves fueled and aflame. Be alert servants of the Master, cheerfully expectant. Don't quit in hard times; pray all the harder. Help needy Christians; be inventive in hospitality.

Bless your enemies; no cursing under your breath. Laugh with your happy friends when they're happy; share tears when they're down. Get along with each other; don't be stuck-up. Make friends with nobodies; don't be the great somebody. (The Message)

ANALYSIS	**15–20 MINUTES**

4. John Stott feels that this passage describes "the apostle's recipe for love" which has "twelve components."[2] These twelve components (in Stott's translation) are as follows:

   1. Sincerity (v. 9a)
   2. Discernment (v. 9b)
   3. Affection (v. 10a)
   4. Honor (v. 10b)
   5. Enthusiasm (v. 11)
   6. Patience (v. 12)
   7. Generosity (v. 13a)
   8. Hospitality (v. 13b)
   9. Good will (v. 14)
   10. Solidarity (v. 15)
   11. Harmony (v. 16a)
   12. Humility (v. 16b)

   In what way does each of these attitudes or actions define what love is and how it operates in a Christian community?

5. If you were to define the meaning of *agape*-love from this passage alone, what overall definition would you come up with?

---

2. Stott, *Romans*, 330.

APPLICATION 15–20 MINUTES

6. Describe a Christian community to which you have belonged (or do belong). Assess the relational life in that community on the basis of what Paul says here about how it should be characterized.

   - What did the community get right?
   - What aspects of community life needed work?
   - What did you contribute to community life?

7. Pick the one aphorism (e.g., *Rejoice in hope*) from Paul's description of love that speaks to your life-situation at this moment in time and explain why this is the case.

8. Where are you in your own growth when it comes to the goals identified in this passage:

   - making love the center of your relational life?
   - letting love prevail in the Christian community of which you are a part?
   - living out each of the twelve parts of love?

9. End this section by reading aloud again *The Message* paraphrase of this passage. Peterson makes this passage wonderfully vivid and very clear in its meaning.

PRAYER 5–15 MINUTES

In your prayer together, focus on a series of the sayings extracted from Romans 12:9–16. With your eyes closed and minds focused on God, listen as your leader reads aloud the passage below twice. As he or she reads, listen for the words or phrase from this selection that resonates with you. In the silence that follows, meditate on those words or phrase. What is God saying to you? How do these words or phrase connect with your life? When the silent meditation ends, join in prayer together offering back to God what you have been thinking and feeling in your meditation.

> *Let love be genuine. Hate what is evil. Love one another with mutual affection. Outdo one another in showing honor. Rejoice in hope. Be patient in suffering. Persevere in prayer. Do not be haughty. Associate with the lowly. Do not claim to be wiser than you are.*

REFLECTION During the week

10. Think about these 12 characteristics of love. Try to define what each looks like in the context of a particular relationship that you have.

11. Now reflect on which characteristics come easiest to you? Which are difficult for you? How can you use your strengths for the sake of the community? How can you grow in areas that are hard for you?

BIBLE STUDY NOTES

Overview

The style in this passage is different from what we have seen thus far in Romans. This is not a reasoned argument as much as it is a series of short, pithy, loosely connected exhortations about how to get along with people. At first glance it may seem as if Paul focuses first on relationships between Christians (vv. 9–13) and then on relationships with those outside the church (vv. 14–16). But, in fact, he probably was thinking of the church during this whole passage (as his use three-times of the phrase "one another" indicates). As much as we would like it to be true, we do not always get along with everyone in our church community so even verse 14 is about life amongst Christians (*Bless those who persecute you*). However, having said this, it is probably also true that Paul would have us apply these same principles of love to all men and women, regardless of how they view Jesus.

This is really an essay on love. Love is the controlling theme. Each aphorism has to do with what love looks like in actual practice. Stott points out that "the apostle's recipe for love" given in these verses has "twelve components."[3] These will be identified in the comments that follow with some changes from Stott's original list.

Verse 9

Context

The main focus in verses 9–16 is on *love* so it is important to be clear about the meaning of this word since it is capable of being defined in so many different ways. The word used here for *love* is the well-known Greek word *agape*. *Agape* refers to self-giving action done on behalf of others (whether they are friends or enemies) made possible by God's Spirit. It is often contrasted to other Greek words for love such as *philia*, which is love for family or *eros*, which is erotic love. In the New Testament *agape*-love is at the heart of what it means to be a follower of Jesus. The Great Commandment is to love God and others (based on accurate self-love). The first thing Paul says about this love (here in verse 9) is that it must be *genuine* (sincere, not counterfeit or showy, without hypocrisy). It is possible to pretend (even to one's self) to love others. John Calvin wrote: "It is difficult to express how ingenious almost all [people] are in counterfeiting a love which they do

3. Ibid., 330.

not really possess. They deceive not only others, but also themselves, while they persuade themselves that they have a true love for those whom they not only treat with neglect, but also, in fact, reject."[4] Paul follows his call to love with, surprisingly, a call to *hate*. What we are to hate is evil. Evil works against love. But this is not just a negative call since Paul then calls us to *hold fast* (cling, be bonded to like glue) to what is good (which stands in opposition to evil). Stott feels that the call in verse 9b is for *discernment* (which is the second thing that Paul says about love): knowing how to distinguish between evil and good. *Sincerity* and *discernment* are the first and second characteristics of love.

Connection

It is already evident that the kind of love to which we are called is not a soft, sentimental feeling. Instead, it is a love that needs to flow from the center of our beings. Without "sincerity," *agape* can feel to the other party like some sort of superior, obligatory benevolence rather than something from the heart.

Furthermore, to love means making choices: choices against that which is evil and choices for that which is good. Love is not an isolated act. It takes places in a moral universe. It needs to flow from the good and not be tainted by the evil.

Verse 10

Context

In this verse the focus is on family affection. Two key words are used: *philostorgos* (*be devoted*) and *philadelphia* (*brotherly/sisterly love*), both of which refer to the natural bonds that occur in families. In this way Paul is reminding us that the Christian community is, at its root, a family and that we should display family warmth and care for one another. The second half of the verse extends this image. Not only should there be mutual affection but mutual honor. This phrase can be translated in two different ways: "esteem others more highly than yourself" as in Philippians 2:3 or as "outdo one another in showing honor." Such honor is easy to show when we remember that each of our brothers and sisters are in union with Christ. Christ is mysteriously present in them.[5] *Affection* and *honor* are the third and fourth characteristics of love.

4. Cranfield, *Romans*, 631.
5. Cranfield, *Romans*, 632–633.

Connection

The context for this love is the family. *Agape* is not something that springs out of the blue. Rather, it comes in the context of mutual affection and mutual respect—the sort of attitudes that characterize the best of families.

Verse 11

Context

Zeal was amongst the most prized attitudes in first-century Judaism. *Ardent* is a Greek word used of boiling water or red-hot metal. Both words describe a strong enthusiasm for the faith. But what is the line between taking faith seriously and taking it too seriously and becoming a fanatic? Paul inserts three qualifiers that serve as checks. First, he has already written that zeal must be based on knowledge (Rom 10:2) and in this chapter he has urged a renewed mind (12:2). Second, the *ardor* is that of the Holy Spirit. Some translations render this phrase "aglow with the Spirit." Third, both zeal and ardor are in the context of serving the Lord, least such energy become excessive and turn into unbridled fanaticism (which serves a cause and not the Lord). What this says in the context of love is that we must be passionate about our loving. Love is not to be an incidental or unenthusiastic way of life. It is to be charged by the attitude of zeal and the ardor of the Spirit, and be in the context of serving the Lord. *Enthusiasm* is the fifth characteristic of love.

Connection

Zeal and ardor are not always words that we use positively when it comes to religion. To be a zealot or fanatic can be very dangerous. One only has to look at all the religious wars—past and present. On the other hand, the danger most of us face is just the opposite: that our faith is peripheral to how we live. A little zeal wouldn't hurt us, much less spiritual ardor! How do we generate zeal? This is a gift from the Lord and an outcome of vital, immediate experience of God.

Verse 12

Context

To the attitudes of zeal and ardor Paul adds three others: *joy*, *patience*, and *perseverance*. The three connect together. It is our joyous hope in our secure inheritance that will be ours in the age to come that makes it possible to endure afflictions and persevere in prayer. Our regularity in prayer, in turn, opens us up to joyous hope and patience in trial. *Joy-filled patience and faithfulness* are the sixth characteristic of love.

Connection

Love must be practiced within the reality of the lives we lead, that is, in the midst of joy and of affliction, with hope and with pain, when times are easy and when times are hard. This is how we meet others: not as perfect people who easily offer care for the needy but as people who know both pain and joy and who need to receive love as well as to offer love.

Verse 13

Context

Sharing is a concrete example of *agape*. *Generosity* of time and resources is the seventh mark of love. *Hospitality* is another concrete example of *agape*. Opening one's home to a stranger was a characteristic of first century Christianity (and the eighth mark of love).

Connection

Generosity and hospitality are especially incumbent upon those of us living in the United States who have so much in comparison to virtually everyone else in the world today.

Verse 14

Context

Stott suggests that our persecutors are outside the Christian community and that this comment anticipates the next section of Romans (verses 17–21). But persecution can also come from within the beloved community. Our posture to those who would be our enemies (whoever they may be) is to be that of blessing (not cursing), i.e., praying for them and acting in a positive way to them. It is Jesus who told us to love our enemies. This command helps us understand the nature of *agape*. It is action done on behalf of others—even enemies. *Good will* is the ninth mark of love.

Connection

We cannot avoid enemies. That is not the issue. The issue is how we respond to them. Our natural response is to give back in kind all the negative input we get from those who dislike us. Paul counsels exactly the opposite response. Learning to live this way is the challenge.

Verse 15

Context

Love shows itself in the sympathy we express to others during times of trial and pain and the joy we share with them during times of celebration. To love is to enter deeply into the experience of the human condition of the other. Presumably such identification with others ought to mark our response to both our friends and our enemies. *Solidarity with the experience of others* is the tenth mark of love.

Connection

Agape love is no disembodied do-gooderism. It flourishes at the heart of the human experience. This is why to become more "spiritual" is to become more "human." God is in the ordinary events of life.

Verse 16

Context

The focus here, in the Greek, is on the mind (as it is in the whole chapter). The call is to "be of the same mind" or "like-minded." *Harmony* is the concrete expression of a common mind, i.e., a common understanding of things. The Christian community is meant to be a place of harmony, not a place of contention. Paul then goes on to identify one of the attitudes that would lead to disharmony: *snobbery*. To think of others in relationship to your own "place" in the scheme of things is to create barriers. Upper, lower, rich, poor, educated, illiterate, "in," "out"—are all names for the ways we set ourselves over others. These are not attitudes of love. *Harmony* and *humility* are the eleventh and twelfth marks of love.

Connection

Despite what Paul calls us to be, the church has often been seen more like a war zone than a haven of harmony.

Summary

The twelve aspects of love are now evident. They define for us what the word *agape* is all about. They also give us a clear goal in our lives: to learn to love in this kind of way. The twelve aspects are:

1. Sincerity (12:9a)
2. Discernment (12:9b)
3. Affection (12:10a)
4. Honor (12:10b)
5. Enthusiasm (12:11)
6. Joy-filled patience and faithfulness (12:12)
7. Generosity (12:13a)
8. Hospitality (12:13b)
9. Good will (12:14)
10. Solidarity (12:15)
11. Harmony (12:16a)
12. Humility (12:16b)

Looking over this list, who can claim to have mastered love? Clearly most everyone has a long way to go. These twelve words give us a clear goal for the kind of transformation that needs to take place in our lives.

SESSION SEVEN

Confession

Bringing Others into the Process of Change

OVERVIEW

The word "confession" has a negative ring to it for most of us. To confess, we think, is to admit we've done wrong and then accept the consequences for our misdeeds. But this is not how confession works in the transformation process. Confession is the act of sharing with another (or others) the issue or problem that binds us. By so doing we invite others to participate with us in our transformation. When we name a problem in this way we also mute its power by bringing it up from the darkness into the light. In this session we are going to explore the role of confession in the transformational process.

Unison Prayer

Pray together a prayer of confession from the Anglican *Book of Common Prayer*.

Almighty God, our heavenly Father,
　we have sinned against you and against our fellow [human beings],
　　in thought and word and deed,
　　　through negligence, through weakness,
　　　　through our own deliberate fault.
We are truly sorry
　and repent of all our sins.
　　for the sake of your Son Jesus Christ, who died for us,
　　　forgive us all that is past;
　　and grant that we may serve you in newness of life;
　　　to the glory of your name. Amen[1]

1. Appleton, *Oxford Book of Prayer*, 245.

SPIRITUAL TRANSFORMATION

OPEN   20–30 MINUTES

"I confess to you . . ."

Confession is not just negative, i.e., describing what you have done wrong. It is also positive, i.e., telling others the good things in your heart. Today's *Open* exercise focuses on the latter kind of confession.

1. "Confess" what you like best so far about this whole small group experience:

   ☐ the opportunity to be with people of like mind
   ☐ the opportunity to do Bible study together
   ☐ the opportunity to be open with one another
   ☐ the opportunity to work on growth issues
   ☐ the opportunity to pray together
   ☐ the opportunity to discuss together
   ☐ the opportunity to wrestle with tough issues together
   ☐ the opportunity to learn new things about being a follower of Jesus
   ☐ other _____

2. "Confess" the misgivings you might have had in joining the group:

   ☐ that I would not get along with the group members
   ☐ that I would be forced to share what I did not want to share
   ☐ that I would not understand what was going on
   ☐ that I would be bored
   ☐ that I would not agree with the perspectives of others
   ☐ that I would fall asleep
   ☐ that I would _____

3. "Confess" one thing you have appreciated about the people in this small group.

CONSIDER　　　　　　　　　　　　　　　15–20 MINUTES

Confession is really an aspect of repentance. Confession is the public part of repentance in which our decision to change moves from the inner realm (our private decision) to the outer realm (our public sharing). We tell another person (or other people) what we have come to see about ourselves and how we want to change. As such, confession is very important. Otherwise repentance remains interior and the dynamics of change are muted due to our inability to bring others into the process.

The Names of Sin

In order to share our problem with another person we need a name for it. In fact, there is great power just in giving a name to the problem. As long as the problem remains in the mists of darkness without much shape or form, it continues to have power over us. But when we bring it into the light, by calling it for what it is, that power begins to diminish. The fact is that unless we come to the point where we look squarely at an issue and name it for what it is, we probably will not grow. It is that simple.

The Bible gives us many names for the various sins that beset us. The Ten Commandments urge us: 1) to have no other gods, 2) not to make graven images of God, 3) not to take God's name in vain, 4) to remember the Sabbath and keep it holy, 5) to honor our father and mother, 6) not to kill, 7) not to commit adultery, 8) not to steal, 9) not to bear false witness against our neighbor, and 10) not to covert our neighbor's goods or spouse. These are foundational issues that define for us what we should and should not do.

In the New Testament Jesus gives us the Great Commandment. We are to love God and to love others using proper self-love as the gauge by which to measure our love. So sin is the failure to love in one of its many forms.

In post New Testament times there was concern about the so-called *Seven Deadly Sins* (that inhibited us in walking the way of love). The original list (which actually had eight items) named the sins of envy, anger, pride, sloth, avarice, gluttony, vainglory, and lust. Later on others sins such as fornication and dejection were added. Gandhi talked about the *Seven Deadly Social Sins*: politics without principle, wealth without work, commerce without morality, pleasure without conscience, education without character, science without humanity, and worship without sacrifice. And in 2008 the Vatican promulgated a list of the *New Deadly Sins*: bioethical violations, morally dubious experiments (e.g. stem cell research), drug abuse, polluting the environment, contributing to the rich/poor divide, excessive wealth, and creating poverty.

Karl Menniger, the well-known psychiatrist, catalogued a whole variety of sins. He speaks of sin manifested as pride (the pride of power, the pride of knowledge, and the pride of virtue); the sins of sensuality (lust, fornication, adultery, and pornography); the sin of gluttony (food, drinks, and drugs); the sins of anger, violence, and aggression; the sin of sloth (laziness, indifference, inactivity, unresponsiveness); the sins of envy, greed, avarice, and affluence; the sin of waste; the sins of cheating and stealing; the sin of lying; and the sin of cruelty.[2] If all this is not enough you can add names like cheating, deception, arrogance, unfaithfulness, dishonesty, embezzlement, hypocrisy, exploitation, injustice to others, hatred, vindictiveness, and bigotry as well as racism, sexism, and fanaticism.

Most of these terms have to do with willful disobedience: doing what we know to be wrong. There are far fewer terms for failure. But the fact is, we do miss the mark in so many ways. We fail to love fully. (A failure to love lies behind so many of our issues in life.) We fail to see clearly what is happening in our lives. We fail to live up to our God-given potential. We fail to use our gifts. We fail to respond to the need of others. We fail to notice God. We have a failure of nerve, a failure of compassion, a failure of energy, a failure of courage, etc. The list goes on.

Then there are all the *lacks* that afflict us: the lack of insight, the lack of love; the lack of compassion, the lack of motivation, the lack of sensitivity, the lack of civility, etc. There are all the relational sins: impatience, anger, jealousy, judgment, haughtiness, condescension, etc.

The point in all this is not the name, per se, but accurate identification of areas in our lives where growth is needed. The "names" simply serve as a grid by which to understand our particular issues. And also, they do allow us to say precisely what troubles us.

The Power of Denial

We begin by naming the problem to ourselves and to God. But this can be surprisingly hard to do. It is not so bad when it comes to ordinary issues like fudging the facts in a story we related to a friend or playing games on the computer when we were supposed to be writing a report. We can own up to this sort of peccadillo—usually. No big consequences, of course. But

---

2. Menninger, *Whatever Became of Sin?*, 133–172.

major stuff like our persistent arrogance or our infidelity—this is hard to admit. "Not me" we cry out, as if keeping it in the dark will make it go away.

When it comes to the act of confession itself, we often find ourselves resisting. We do not want to do it. It is okay to admit you are a sinner like everybody else but to name the specific sin—well that is different. "That is not really necessary is it?" we ask ourselves. We pull back. We want to talk about something else. Our attention wanders.

This is denial rearing its ugly head. Denial is the refusal to admit to having a particular problem. Denial is covering up, hiding, avoiding the issue, and pretending it does not exist. Anything but confession. "I can't say the words. I'm not like that," we say to ourselves.

Denial comes in many shapes and forms:

- *Avoidance*: "I refusal to talk about the problem."
- *Blame*: "If my wife didn't nag me so much I'd spend more time at home and not work so much."
- *Rationalization*: "The reason I overspent again was that the store was having such a fantastic sale. It would have been foolish not to take advantage of it."
- *Excusing*: "I was tired and I needed a break and television is relaxing to me."
- *Minimizing*: "Looking at pornography is not that bad."
- *Comparing*: "I'm not like Alec. Now he has a real problem with drinking."
- *Covering Up*: "If I hide my raise from my husband I'll have some extra money for myself."
- *Explaining*: "You just caught me on a bad day. I don't usually eat this much ice cream."
- *Delaying*: "I know I've got to stop smoking. I'm going to do it for Lent."
- *Plain denial*: "I don't have a problem."

It is hard to get through denial to reality. In fact, it sometimes takes a trained professional to get behind our denial. But mostly it takes a sense on our part that God loves us and wants us to grow, that God's posture toward us is one of forgiveness and not condemnation, and that unless we own up we will stay stuck—and this harms us.

The Power of Others[3]

But why confess our shortcomings to others? Why not keep these problems to ourselves? Certainly our instinct is toward secrecy and hiddenness.

There are several principles at work here. For one thing, naming an issue puts the problem into the public arena. And once it is out there in view of others we have a kind of commitment to do something about it. Even if others do not hold us to account (by reminding us that we said we were going to work on an issue), we still feel accountable. We need to do something; we need to get on with it. Second, our friends will hold us accountable (if we let them)! They will assist us (as they able) in dealing with the issue. They will listen to us as we wrestle with the problem. They will pray with us and for us. Change was never meant to be a private struggle. It was always meant to be a communal process. As they assist us, so we assist them with their issues. Mutual accountability. That is what the Christian community is all about: a clinic for recovering sinners in which we all help each other to be conformed to the image of Christ. It is not surprising that St. James urges us to "confess your sins to each other and pray for each other so that you may be healed" (Jas 5:16).

To whom do we name our issue? Certainly we need to name it to ourselves and to God. Sometimes this is enough. We sense God's forgiveness, guidance, and power. We go from strength to strength as we move away from the old behavior, attitude, or idea to the new behavior, attitude, or idea. But at other times this is not enough. We need to name the issue to an appropriate other. Who that might be varies. Certainly we owe the most honesty to those closest to us: spouse, then children, then family, then friends—and so the circles of openness radiate outward. Interestingly, we sometimes reverse the whole process. The anonymous bartender or hair stylist hears the most. Presumably their remoteness from our daily lives gives us safety in disclosure.

Sometimes we may need professional help—a pastoral counselor, a therapist, or another trained professional who can help us get at what is going on in our lives. At other times it is the person who you have offended

---

3. For a striking and illuminating discussion of the power of public confession see Molly Phinney Baskette's book, *Standing Naked Before God: The Art of Public Confession*. Each week, in her growing church, someone stands up and "tells about a time they messed up, broke bad, or made Jesus want to cry."

(or harmed) who must be consulted and to whom the confession is owed (as long as you do not harm that person by so doing). At still other times a small group of caring others with whom you are in an accountable relationship need to be the ones who hear your story. Sometimes, if the sin was public (or impacted the public), the confession needs to be more general.

The principle is clear: we need to move our repentance from within to without and so gain the strength needed to change that comes from compassionate care given us by others who know what we are struggling with.

DISCUSSION   10–15 MINUTES

4. How does naming an issue help a person to deal with that issue?

5. Discuss the long list of names above, drawn from the Bible (and elsewhere), for those transgressions and failings that afflict us as human beings. Which name stood out to you? Why? What other names can you add to this long list?

6. Which of the many forms of denial listed above (if any) is most familiar to you?

7. How does confession assist us in the transformation process? Discuss the pros and cons of confession.

APPLICATION   10–15 MINUTES

Continue the conversation that you began in Session Five about the issues you are confronting at this point in your life. You may wish to split up into the same sub-groups of four in order to give yourselves more time for conversation.

8. Focus on the central question: *At this moment in time, what is the name of issue with which you wrestle?*

   - What is your story?
   - What is the problem?
   - How does it impact you?
   - Where are you in dealing with it?

How open you are willing and able to be will depend upon the group you are in and on how much you have come to trust one another. Suffice it to say, your small group is an ideal context within which to deal with the tough issues of growth. But share only what you are comfortable sharing. Remember that all sharing is confidential and so kept within the group itself.

PRAYER   5–10 MINUTES

End this small group session with a time of prayer in which you ask God for:

- the ability to name your issue
- the power to overcome denial
- the willingness to confess in ways that are appropriate
- the power of God to deal with your real life issues

REFLECTION   During the week

9. Copy out in your journal, one by one, the many names for transgression and failure listed above. As you do so, pay attention to those names that catch your attention, even if you don't know why. Circle them for further reflection.

10. Pick one of these circled words and reflect on why it might have meaning for you. How do you experience it? How does it inhibit you in walking in the way of love? What might you do about this?

Session Eight

Service not Retaliation

A Bible Study on Romans 12:17–21

OVERVIEW

So far Paul's focus has been on relationships within the Christian community. Now it shifts to the question of how one treats those who make themselves your enemies because you are a Christian. What he counsels is radical: non-retaliation and service toward those who persecute you. Such a stance is only possible through the transforming power of Jesus Christ.

Unison Prayer

Begin with a prayer for one's enemies that was written in the 15th century.

> *O God, if there are those who wish evil for me or do evil and are my enemies and are my opponents and persecutors, grant to them, O Lord, indulgence and eternal rest, and bring them to your will. Lord, deign to convert their hearts to wholesome peace, to turn all the malice which they plot secretly or wish against me into good. Grant me your mercy and save me so that unharmed I might be able to thwart their every effort; and . . . also, that I may be able to love a friend in you, and an enemy for your sake. Amen.*[1]

OPEN   20–30 MINUTES

Enemies

Okay, so we are supposed to love everybody but, in fact, there are people we do not like. Whether we actually call them "enemies," we certainly do not rank them amongst our favorite people. Who are the negative people in your world?

1. Appleton, *Oxford Book of Prayer*, 111.

1. When you were a kid, who were your favorite villains?
   - ❐ Comic book characters like the Joker
   - ❐ Communists
   - ❐ Evil aliens
   - ❐ Republicans
   - ❐ Democrats
   - ❐ Crooks and other bad guys on television
   - ❐ Athletes on opposing sports teams
   - ❐ Others: _____

2. When you were at school, was there anybody who bullied you or hassled you? Who didn't like you at school? Who didn't you like? Why?

3. What is your method of choice when it comes to peace making?
   - ❐ Saying you are sorry   ❐ Pretending it never happened
   - ❐ Making him/her say "I'm sorry"   ❐ Avoiding the person
   - ❐ Seeking consensus   ❐ Offering forgiveness
   - ❐ Avoiding conflict in the first place
   - ❐ Baking cookies for him/her

THE PASSAGE   5 MINUTES

To follow Christ is to follow him not just in church but also out in the world where we spend most of our time. However, the world around us is not always open to the non-conformity of the Christian. In fact, at times it is openly hostile. Paul experienced this. His remarks in this section of Romans about how to treat those who are your enemies because of your faith are not merely theoretical. At the point in history when he wrote this letter, the church was beginning to experience harassment. A few years later the Roman government would actively start to persecute Christians.

Read aloud the following passage in both translations.

Service not Retaliation

Romans 12:17–21

17Do not repay anyone evil for evil, but take thought for what is noble in the sight of all. 18If it is possible, so far as it depends on you, live peaceably with all. 19Beloved, never avenge yourselves, but leave room for the wrath of God; for it is written, "Vengeance is mine, I will repay, says the Lord." 20No, "if your enemies are hungry, feed them; if they are thirsty, give them something to drink; for by doing this you will heap burning coals on their heads." 21Do not be overcome by evil, but overcome evil with good. (NRSV)

Don't hit back; discover beauty in everyone. If you've got it in you, get along with everybody. Don't insist on getting even; that's not for you to do. "I'll do the judging," says God. "I'll take care of it."

Our Scriptures tell us that if you see your enemy hungry, go buy that person lunch, or if he's thirsty, get him a drink. Your generosity will surprise him with goodness. Don't let evil get the best of you; get the best of evil by doing good. (The Message)

ANALYSIS   15–20 MINUTES

4. What are the three prohibitions that Paul gives us in this section?

   - Do not _____
   - Do not _____
   - Do not _____

5. What are the four positive responses we are to make instead?

   - _____
   - _____
   - _____
   - _____

6. Discuss how it is that non-retaliation and active service of others defuses hostility, anger, and persecution. Discuss the challenge of living in a non-retaliatory way. This is not easy!

7. As you look out on the world, where would you locate active evil? Persistent good?

APPLICATION   15–20 MINUTES

8. Who are your enemies? (It is important to name them with some clarity otherwise this section remains merely theoretical. Do not worry about the cause of their hostility or whether your opposition to them is justified or not, just name those with whom you have profound disagreement. This may involve disagreement over politics, morality, social action, etc. or it may be more personal having to do with enemies at work, in the church or community, or in your family.) Be prepared to discuss one such person (who can remain anonymous) with the group. How does this passage help you in your relationship with that person?

9. Can you recall an experience in which non-retaliation and active good directed at the other brought about peace and resolution? If so, share the incident with the group.

10. In what situations might you be called upon to act as a peacemaker? How does this passage help you in this role?

11. What is the danger of labeling others as enemies? To whom might you appear to be an enemy? Why?

12. End this section by reading aloud again *The Message* paraphrase of this passage.

PRAYER 5–15 MINUTES

In your prayer together, focus on the Romans 12:17–18. With your eyes closed and minds focused on God, listen as your leader reads aloud the passage below twice. As he or she reads, listen for the words or phrase from this selection that resonates with you. In the silence that follows, meditate on those words or phrase. What is God saying to you? How do these words or phrase connect with your life? When the silent meditation ends, join in prayer together offering back to God what you have been thinking and feeling in your meditation.

> *Do not repay anyone evil for evil, but take thought for what is noble in the sight of all. If it is possible, so far as it depends on you, live peaceably with all.*

REFLECTION During the week

13. Think about those whom you do not like. Who are your enemies and why? Make a list in your journal of all those with whom you have broken relationships. Include not just the present but also the past. What soured these relationships?

14. Reflect on how you might restore some of these relationships. What would non-retaliation and service look like in these relationships?

BIBLE STUDY NOTES
Overview

How we treat others is an important part of our public life and witness. How we respond when we are mistreated is especially important. First-century Christians were often persecuted for their faith, even to the point of death in some instances. In this context of persecution Paul urges Christians not to retaliate, even though such a response might be justified. Instead he calls them to active service of their enemies. Non-retaliation and service are important parts of their (and our) public life.

Paul has already anticipated this topic when in verse 14 he talked about those who persecute us. Here his focus is on evildoers. In each case he forbids retaliation and revenge. He repeats this prohibition in four places:

- "Do not curse them" (those who persecute you) (verse 14)
- "Do not repay anyone evil for evil" (verse 17)
- "Never avenge yourselves" (verse 19)
- "Do not be overcome by evil" (verse 21)

For each prohibition there is a positive counterpart:

- "Bless those who persecute you" (verse 14)
- "Take thought for what is noble in the sight of all . . . live peaceably with all" (verses 17–18)
- "Leave room for the wrath of God" (verse 19)
- "Overcome evil with good" (verse 21)

Behind this stance of non-retaliation is the model of Jesus who did not bring vengeance on his enemies, instead he allowed himself to be crucified. Jesus' example is in line with his teaching. See especially the Sermon on the Mount (Matthew 5–7).

The focus in this section is on personal conduct when it comes to evildoers. In the next section (13:1–7) Paul will examine the responsibilities of the government and the courts in dealing with evildoers.

Verse 17

Context

We are not to retaliate by responding to evil with evil on our part. Evil is not a tool of the follower of Jesus. But Paul does not stop with the negative: do not retaliate. He takes the next step and urges a positive response. We are to practice good (not evil). This was a view that was common to the early church (see 1 Thess 5:15 and 1 Pet 3:4). The good that we are to practice is a kind of common morality that is recognized as such by all who are involved. J. B. Phillips translates this: "See that your public behavior is above criticism."

Connection

Paul knows us well. When harmed, our first desire is to harm the perpetrator. They hurt us, and so we feel justified in bringing vengeance to bear on them. Knowing this all too human tendency, Paul launches this section by immediately forbidding us to give in to the temptation to repay evil with evil. With that option no longer open to us, we have to listen with some care as to how we are meant to respond to our enemies.

What Christians are called upon to do is not just what the consensus calls "good," but those things that are inherently "good." Such actions will be recognized as such by all people of good will.

Verse 18

Context

Paul does not stop by urging us to practice "good." Here he tells us we are also to be peacemakers. We are to take the next step. Not only must we refuse to respond to others in negative ways (in this way we do not inflame an argument), we must reach out to them to make peace (and so turn the argument into good). Notice, however, that Paul offers two qualifications to his imperative. We are to be peacemakers "if it is possible" and "as far as it depends on you." He recognizes that peace is not always possible because the other party may not be open to peace.

Connection

Peacemaking is a vital need in the world today. This section of Romans gives us practical help in being such a person. The whole idea of not retaliating, but responding to the needs of the other, is a potent insight. The great

Methodist missionary E. Stanley Jones recounts examples of how such an attitude of non-retaliation and service brings peace (e.g. see his spiritual autobiography, *A Song of Ascents*). It makes sense when we think about it. When we retaliate, even when it might be commonly felt that we were more than justified to do so, we simply keep the problem going. Our retaliation begets retaliation from the other person and so the problem escalates. But if we refuse to play that game, and instead absorb that which is directed at us rather than giving it back, we break the cycle. If, in addition, we reach out in a positive way with the welfare of the other in mind, we make it most difficult for there to be further hostility. But, alas, this is easier said than done and as Paul notes, others can rebuff our efforts at peacemaking.

Verse 19

Context

It is God who deals with evil, not us. This is Paul's point in this verse. Evil needs to be dealt with but it is not our job to do so, thus we must not retaliate or take revenge. Paul addresses his readers as "beloved." All of this is said in the context of love: Paul's love for them and Jesus' call for us as his disciples to love all people.

Connection

It is very hard not to take justice into our own hands. Again, Paul knows this. He can picture us burning with righteous indignation that leads us to take out after the evil other. In the next section of his letter he will reflect on the role of government in punishing evil. This verse presupposes the existence of a moral universe in which good and evil exist but where evil is dealt with. It is this view of the world that enables us to leave justice in the hands of others and to know that in the end, good will win out. Without such a vision of reality, it will be impossible not to take justice into our own hands.

Verse 20

Context

Instead of revenge we are called to service. If our enemy needs food or drink, we are to provide it for him or her. This is a concrete example of the kind of response we are called upon to make. Such actions fit exactly into the definition of *agape*-love, which is good done on behalf of the other regardless of how we might feel about that other person.

Just what this most vivid image of "heaping burning coals on his head" is all about is difficult to know exactly. Some would say that providing kindness of every sort to one's enemies may induce a kind of inner shame that leads to repentance and hence to reconciliation and true friendship. According to Stott, more recent research points to "an ancient Egyptian ritual in which a penitent would carry burning coals on his head as evidence of the reality of his repentance. In this case the coals are 'a dynamic symbol of change of mind which takes place as a result of a deed of love.'"[2] Certainly, such acts of good are meant to lead the other into the kingdom of God and away from the power of evil.

Connection

The call to service is an amazing admonition since again it goes against our natural instincts. Once more Paul is counseling us to become something different from what we would be if we were left to our own devices. Christian transformation is all about becoming new creatures in Christ Jesus.

Verse 21

Context

The contrast between good and evil that appears throughout this section (e.g., 12:9, 17, 21; 13:1–4) is stated clearly in this verse. There is no middle ground. If we give into the acts of evil which Paul prohibits (curse, repay evil with evil, take revenge) then we have moved into the sphere of evil. Evil will have overcome us. Whereas, if we act as he urges us to do (bless, do the right thing, live at peace, leave vengeance to God) we will overcome evil and the good will have prevailed.

Connection

We do not talk much about good and evil these days. It seems too simplistic given the complexity and ambiguity of the postmodern world. We are far more comfortable with the gray rather than with the black and white. It is true that much of life falls into the middle zone where the good is tainted by the bad and where it is difficult to discern on which side the angels would cast their vote. Still, we dare not lose our vision of good and evil and so plunge into a morally ambiguous universe where the right is whatever we happen to think or do. Perhaps it is in our desire for retaliation that we can

---

2. Stott, *Romans*, 336..

locate the nature of evil—in us and not in others. We need to be aware of our own tendencies to evil (against which Paul warns us) and to learn a new way in the face of them.

Session Nine

Faith

The Resources that Bring about Change

OVERVIEW

Repentance alone does not bring about change. It only signals the willingness to change. It is when repentance is paired with faith that transformation emerges. It is faith that activates the spiritual resources that result in change. Strictly speaking, faith does not itself bring into being these resources. Faith is a word that describes how we reach out in trust to take hold of that which is already there for us: the love and power of God and others. In this session we will look at how repentance and faith together produce transformation.

Unison Prayer

Pray together a prayer by S. C. Hughson that focuses on our need for faith.
> Lord, I believe you are the way, the truth and the life.
> Make me so to walk with you that by you I may come to the Father;
>> make my faith strong to believe all that you have revealed,
>>> for you are the very truth.
>
> Give me your life that I may say, "I live, yet not I, but Christ lives in me;"
>> by your divine omnipotence direct and strengthen my faith,
>> by your divine wisdom instruct and enlighten it,
>> by your divine goodness sustain and perfect it,
> that I may abide in you unchanging to the end. Amen.[1]

---

1. Appleton, *Oxford Book of Prayer*, 90.

SPIRITUAL TRANSFORMATION

OPEN — 20–30 MINUTES

Naive or Not

Where do you rank on the "I believe you" scale?

1. When you get a phone call from a tele-marketer, what do you tend to do?

   ☐ hang up immediately

   ☐ listen for a while and then hang up

   ☐ listen to the whole spiel and then hang up

   ☐ listen to the whole spiel and buy the product (or give the money)

2. When you read something in an article that is strange, amazing, or unexpected, how do you react?

   ☐ I dismiss it as "journalistic license"

   ☐ I think about it

   ☐ I try to get other information to confirm or deny it

   ☐ I share it with others as true

   ☐ I share it with other as false

   ☐ I like strange events

   ☐ I like ordinary life

3. Where are you on the credulity scale? Why are you this way, do you suppose?

I believe everything	I believe most things	I believe some things	I disbelieve some things	I disbelieve most things	I disbelieve everything

CONSIDER — 15–20 MINUTES

When St. Mark summed up the essence of Jesus' message he put it this way, "The kingdom of God has come near. Repent and believe in the good news" (Mark 1:15). In other words, the response to the dawning of God's kingdom is the two-fold action of repentance and faith (or belief). Repentance says, "Yes, I want to leave behind the kingdom of this world and become a part of the kingdom of God." Faith says, "I will trust in the saving work of Jesus to enable me to become part of God's kingdom." This is the equation for growth: repentance + faith = transformation. Faith is the final element that we need to discuss so as to understand the dynamic of transformation.

The Meaning of Faith

But what is faith? This seems to be an odd question since "faith" is such a well-known word. Unlike the word "repentance," which is seldom used and generally misunderstood, the word "faith" is part of our cultural vocabulary. "Keep the faith," "have faith in me," and "the faith to go on" are all familiar expressions. But herein lies the problem. The word "faith" is so familiar that we are hard-put to define just what it means. And even when we have offered a tentative definition it is likely to be inaccurate or incomplete since the New Testament word "faith" has a meaning that goes well beyond our cultural understanding.

In the New Testament, to have *faith* (the noun) or to *believe* (the verb) has a cognitive, an affective, and a behavioral aspect. In other words, faith is something we hold to be true, something we feel, and something we do. New Testament faith begins with knowledge: we believe that what God says is true. Our minds are convinced. But then our conviction turns into trust. Trust is knowing in our hearts that what we believe is indeed so. Trust is a relational term. It exists between people. We not only believe what God says, we trust the God who says it. Finally, our warm-hearted conviction results in action. We act on the basis of what we believe. Because we know and trust God, we live in a certain way. We follow Jesus. In other words, New Testament faith engages the whole person.

If it is repentance that opens the possibility of change, then it is faith that actually brings about new growth. There are at least three ways in which faith brings about growth. First, faith enables us to face ourselves as we truly are because by faith we know that God loves us and forgives us. Faith provides the spiritual and psychological grounding we need in order to change. Second, faith defines the direction in which our change is to take place. Change in and of itself may be good, bad, or neutral. But Christian transformation involves moving in the direction of God. We trust the Bible to define that direction for us. Third, by faith we access those gifts from God that bring about change such as the gift of guidance, the gift of fellowship, and the gift of the Holy Spirit. I want to explore further each of these three ways in which faith enables growth.

Faith, Love, and Forgiveness

First, faith enables us to face ourselves as we really are. By faith we are assured of two vital facts: that God really does love us and that God will actually forgive us. Knowing this, we have the courage to face what is ugly in ourselves. We can look, without hesitation, at those areas of our life that are in need of redemption. Without this assurance of love and forgiveness, our natural tendency is either to shy away from the sort of input that will point out our weaknesses, or to deny that any problem exists.

Knowing that God loves us and forgives us also provides the incentive to change. When it comes to change we always have to wrestle with a series of questions: Why change? Why bother? What does it matter? Who cares? Well, God apparently cares—cares enough to send Jesus to die for us. When we know how much God loves us, we have a deep desire to become all that God wants us to be. Love begets love. God loves us and so we love God and seek to please God. As Jesus said, "If you love me, you will keep my commandments" (John 14:15).

It is by faith that we know that God loves us. We know this because Jesus, who is God in human flesh, came to our planet. Not only did God love us enough to squeeze himself into the close confines of flesh (the Creator become creature) but Jesus took one infinite step more. He died for us. In dying Jesus took upon himself the entire weight of the moral universe. Singlehandedly he dealt with all the accumulated sin and lostness of humanity from the dawn of time. He made forgiveness possible. All this was done at great personal price—a price that we can scarcely imagine—the Lord of Life given over to death. This is a profound mystery. Jesus did all this because of love. Both the incarnation and the crucifixion are acts of love.

So when we look at Jesus we see a God who loves us, individually and personally. Just so he would make sure we got the point, Jesus told us the story of Prodigal Son (Luke 15:11–31). Within the three characters in this seminal story resides the drama of love. The child who leaves home and squanders his inheritance, the older brother who stays home and becomes resentful, and the father who loves them both—not because of what they have done (in fact, in spite of what they have done!) but because to love is who he is. This is God's love for us.

When we believe that we are loved and forgiven we are freed to grow and change. This is what faith is all about: trust in a loving God who forgives us causes us to live in ways that we would not otherwise be able to live. The power of love is great. It motivates us to become what our loving parent calls us to be, it cleanses us from our sin, it enables us to grow, it reassures us that we are valuable, it keeps us going when the temptation is to stop, it enfolds us in the kind of care that nurtures, it creates a great and good hunger to know the God of love, and it expunges from our hearts the desire to sin.

Faith and Scripture

There is a second way in which faith relates to transformation. *Our faith defines for us the direction in which we ought to change.* It is by faith that we accept that the pattern for living set out in Scripture is indeed God's pattern. In the Bible, we have been given a very concrete idea of the way in which we ought to be living and hence we can seek constantly to adjust our lives in that direction. Without such guidance the nature of our change would be haphazard. We might become aware, for example, that our relationship with our children is in bad shape. We want to change. But how? Without the sort of Scriptural insights into the nature of human relationships in general and into parent and child relationships in particular, the change we initiate might even worsen the situation!

I think we sometimes do not realize how valuable a resource we have, as Christians, in the Scriptures. The insights in the Bible provide us with the insight we need in order to make sense out of this life. This is quite staggering. We are not left to flounder this way and that, trying desperately to discover what brings wholeness to life. The pattern is there. This is not to say that we always act consistently in accord with Scriptural teachings, or even that we have invested enough energy to learn what the Bible actually says. Nevertheless, general life directions are there, and by faith we believe them to be from God and hence we can know in what direction change ought to take place.

Faith and the Gifts of God

There is yet a third way in which faith enables transformation. *By faith we open ourselves to those gifts from God that bring about change: the gift of guidance, the gift of fellowship, and the gift of the Holy Spirit, in particular.*

God has promised us guidance. God *will* lead us, the Bible declares. God has already done this by setting down in Scripture the general patterns for living. But there will come those times when we need a specific word from God. It is then that the "still, small voice" speaking within us makes all the difference.[2]

Very often it is the presence of a fellowshipping community that makes change possible. On our own we are so powerless. We can "will" all sorts of things, but we never seem to have the power actually to do that which we say we desire. Yet, when we participate in a community of caring, sharing, and burden-bearing people we find strength beyond ourselves. This has certainly been the experience of Alcoholic Anonymous groups based on the Twelve Steps, which are drawn from the New Testament.[3]

Finally, there is the gift of the Holy Spirit. It is the Holy Spirit who provides the power that enables us to change. Countless people down through the ages have testified to transformation that has taken place in their lives, brought about by a power they knew was not their own. This is the testimony of alcoholics and drug-dependent individuals who found the power to give up their addiction instantly and forever. This is the testimony of those who find a new ability to love, to forgive, to cope, to hope, or to trust. Not by great effort on their part but simply as a result of an act of faith, they find a new reality present in their lives. All this is the work of the Holy Spirit.

The Function of Faith

How does faith "work"? It is one thing to define it; it is another thing to live it. The answer to this question is found in the definition of faith with which we began. *We believe, we trust, and we act.* Having discerned an issue that troubles us, we offer the problem to God. We ask for forgiveness where that is needed. We trust that God does forgive us. We offer ourselves to God, in the knowledge that we are loved and that we can change. We let Scripture define the direction for our change. We open ourselves to the gifts given us for change. We share the problem with friends. We ask God to guide us. We offer the problem to the Holy Spirit. And we carry on. We trust that God is active in our healing. Each of these actions is separate yet each occurs as part of a whole. To have faith is to open oneself to God, holding the issue in one hand, and reaching out to God with the other hand—knowing as we do this that faith connects us to the living God who loves us and brings about change in us.[4]

---

2. For further insight into this whole issue of listening to God see my book *Noticing God*.

3. See my book *12 Steps: The Path to Wholeness*.

4. Some of the material in this section is adapted from Peace, *Pilgrimage*, 84-93.

DISCUSSION   10–15 MINUTES

4. Discuss the three aspects of New Testament "faith."

   - What is the role of truth in the action of faith?
   - Why is whole-hearted trust so important when it comes to faith?
   - Why is it necessary for us to act upon what we believe?

5. In what ways does God's love and forgiveness produce growth and transformation? What is the role of faith in accessing the love and forgiveness of God?

6. How does repentance and faith produce growth?

APPLICATION   10–15 MINUTES

Continue the conversation begun in session three about areas of growth in your life. You may need to break up into sub-groups of four so as to allow more time for individual sharing. You may need simply to continue the discussion you were having in session seven, now allowing others to share. Or you may want to discuss the step of faith that you are being called to in light of the issue with which you struggle.

7. What is God asking of you and how are you responding?

8. In what ways will faith enable you to deal with your issue?

If you decide to talk in general terms about the dynamic of faith, the following questions can be used:

9. Is it easy or is it hard for you to believe that God loves you and forgives you? Explain. What difference does this fact make in your life?

10. What is your experience of the love of God? How does this impact your own growth?

11. How does Scripture work in your life when it comes to growth?

12. Where are you in your life when it comes to accessing the transforming gifts of God: the gift of guidance, the gift of fellowship, and the gift of the Holy Spirit?

13. What is the prayer you are praying at this point in your life when it comes to growth?

PRAYER   5–10 MINUTES

End this small group session with a time of prayer in which you ask God for:

- a deep understanding of the power of faith
- openness to the guidance of Scripture in your life
- the gifts of guidance, fellowship, and the Holy Spirit

REFLECTION   During the week

During the week, go back over the questions in the *Application* section.

14. Which questions resonate most deeply with you? Why? What is it you need to consider? Journal your responses.

Session Ten

Citizenship

A Bible Study on Romans 13:1–7

OVERVIEW

Down through the centuries there has been an uneasy relationship between Christianity and the political systems of the world. In some times and places, the State has been (at least nominally) Christian. In other times and places, the State has actively persecuted those calling themselves Christians. In the United States at this point in time we are re-examining what separation of church and state entails. In the midst of this reflection, Paul's words to us about the way Christians are to relate to the State are a help and a challenge as we seek to sort out our role as responsible citizens.

Unison Prayer

Begin with a prayer from the Anglican *Book of Common Prayer* (1928).

> *Almighty God, from whom all thoughts of truth and peace proceed: Kindle, we pray, in the hearts of all [people] the true love of peace; and guide with your pure and peaceable wisdom those who take counsel for the nations of the earth; that in tranquility your kingdom may go forward, till the earth is filled with knowledge of your love; through Jesus Christ our Lord. Amen.*[1]

---

1. Appleton, *Oxford Book of Prayer*, 223.

SPIRITUAL TRANSFORMATION

OPEN　　　　　　　　　　　　　　　　　**20–30 MINUTES**

Authority: Good, Bad, and Indifferent

There is always somebody "over us" it seems. When we are kids we are accountable to a whole array of people ranging from parents, teachers, principals, police to adults in general. When we grow up we still have to pay taxes, obey the law, and abide by all the other regulations that "the authorities" have put in place. How well do you cope with authority?

1. When you were a kid, how would you characterize your stance toward authority? Give an illustration if you can.

    ☐ I obeyed　　　☐ I resisted　　　☐ I rebelled

    ☐ I did what I was told　　☐ I made the rules for my gang

    ☐ I obeyed the spirit but not the letter of the law

    ☐ I conformed　　☐ I mostly conformed

    ☐ I sometimes conformed

    ☐ I gave the appearance of obedience

    ☐ I sought ways to get back at the authorities

2. When you were a kid, who was your favorite authority figure and why?

3. In your adult life for whom are you "the person in charge" and how do you feel about this?

THE PASSAGE 5 MINUTES

Read aloud the following passage in both translations.

Romans 13:1-7

1Let every person be subject to the governing authorities; for there is no authority except from God, and those authorities that exist have been instituted by God. 2Therefore whoever resists authority resists what God has appointed, and those who resist will incur judgment. 3For rulers are not a terror to good conduct, but to bad. Do you wish to have no fear of the authority? Then do what is good, and you will receive its approval; 4for it is God's servant for your good. But if you do what is wrong, you should be afraid, for the authority does not bear the sword in vain! It is the servant of God to execute wrath on the wrongdoer. 5Therefore one must be subject, not only because of wrath but also because of conscience. 6For the same reason you also pay taxes, for the authorities are God's servants, busy with this very thing. 7Pay to all what is due them—taxes to whom taxes are due, revenue to whom revenue is due, respect to whom respect is due, honor to whom honor is due. (NRSV)

Be a good citizen. All governments are under God. Insofar as there is peace and order, it's God's order. So live responsibly as a citizen. If you're irresponsible to the state, then you're irresponsible with God, and God will hold you responsible. Duly constituted authorities are only a threat if you're trying to get by with something. Decent citizens should have nothing to fear.

Do you want to be on good terms with the government? Be a responsible citizen and you'll get on just fine, the government working to your advantage. But if you're breaking the rules right and left, watch out. The police aren't there just to be admired in their uniforms. God also has an interest in keeping order, and he uses them to do it. That's why you must live responsibly–not just to avoid punishment but also because it's the right way to live.

That's also why you pay taxes–so that an orderly way of life can be maintained. Fulfill your obligations as a citizen. Pay your taxes, pay your bills, respect your leaders. (The Message)

ANALYSIS 15–20 MINUTES

4. How are Christians to relate to the state?

5. What reasons does Paul give for such a stance?

6. What is the God-given role of the state? How do you respond to the assertion that "the authorities are God's servants"?

7. Discuss ways in which the following three statements from the New Testament fit together and provide a pattern for civil obedience and civil disobedience.

   - Paul in Romans 13:1, defining the basic stance of Christians to the state: "Everyone must submit himself to the governing authorities, for there is no authority except that which God has established."
   - Peter and the other apostles in Acts 5:29 when told by religious officials not to preach about Jesus: "We must obey God rather than men!"
   - Jesus in Mark 12:17 when asked about paying taxes: "Give to Caesar what is Caesar's and to God what is God's."

CITIZENSHIP

APPLICATION   15–20 MINUTES

8. What is your basic view of government? Explain your answer.

    ❐ it is good

    ❐ it is bad

    ❐ it is indifferent

    ❐ it is a mix of good and bad

    ❐ it is corrupt

    ❐ it is God-sent

    ❐ it is in need of renewal

    ❐ it is in need of re-organization

    ❐ it is need of good people to run it

9. What are the reasons that people give for not submitting to the government? Consider issues from the small (speeding) to the large (war).

10. What are the issues on which, potentially, you would oppose the government on the basis of your commitment to God?

11. At what point is your own behavior toward the government (laws, taxes, respect, etc.) challenged by what the New Testament says?

12. If you had lived in South Africa in the days of *Apartheid* when the law made non-whites into second-class citizens with few of the rights and privileges of whites, what might your stance have been toward the government?

13. End this section by reading aloud again *The Message* paraphrase of this passage. Notice how Peterson in his paraphrase seeks to capture a nuanced understanding of how we are to relate to the state.

PRAYER   5–15 MINUTES

In your prayer together, focus on the Romans 13:3–4a. With your eyes closed and minds focused on God, listen as your leader reads aloud the passage below twice. As he or she reads, listen for the words or phrase from this selection that resonates with you. In the silence that follows, meditate on those words or phrase. What is God saying to you? How do these words or phrase connect with your life? When the silent meditation ends, join in prayer together offering back to God what you have been thinking and feeling in your meditation.

> *For rulers are not a terror to good conduct, but to bad. Do you wish to have no fear of the authority? Then do what is good, and you will receive its approval; for it is God's servant for your good.*

REFLECTION   During the week

14. Reflect on your relationship to the government on all levels: national, regional, and local. How does government impinge on your life from the services it provides to the taxes and fees it requires? How do you view all this: as good, bad, or simply the way it is.

15. Are you a good citizen? Muse on this question. How does your faith inform your citizenship?

BIBLE STUDY NOTES
Overview

Paul's continues in this section to discuss how Christians relate to those outside the church, in this case, to the government and those employed by the government. The general principles in Romans 12:17–21 (don't resort to violence to "get even" but serve your enemy) are now given specific focus in this discussion of the relationship of Christians to civil authorities.

To understand properly this passage, historical conditions must be taken into account lest one understands this text to teach more than it does. In Paul's day Rome was clearly a restraining force against chaos. Furthermore, it was crucial that Christians be seen as good citizens so as not to be expelled from Rome as the Jews had been because of a riot some years earlier (probably occasioned by Christ being preached in the synagogue). Note, too, that Paul does *not* deal with the question of how Christians relate to a government gone sour, just as in Romans he doesn't tell Christians how to relate to an apostate church. Nor does he give any guidance as to how Christians should involve themselves in a participatory democracy, which was quite a different governmental system than Rome in the first century. This passage was a specific word to particular Christians in a given era.

Therefore, care must be taken in making twenty-first century applications, especially since in the Book of Revelation Rome, in a later era, is pictured as now having fallen and come under the control of evil (Rev 13:6–7) and so Christians must relate to it quite differently than when it was a force for restraint and the carrying out of God's will. Jesus himself provided the foundational understanding of church-state relationship when he said, "Give to the emperor the things that are the emperor's, and to God the things that are God's" (Mark 12:17). Church and state each have different roles and Christians owe different responses to each. Paul builds on this perspective in this passage.

Verse 1

Context

Christians are called upon to submit to the authority of the ruling powers. The reason for this is that human authority is derived from God's authority. The word "submit" is sometimes mistranslated as "obey" (there are three different Greek words for obedience). Submission here must be understood in light of Romans 12:10 (honoring others above oneself) and Philippians

2:3 (counting others as better). Christians must recognize the claim that the authorities have upon them. But having said this they also have to remember Acts 5:29 where "Peter and the other apostles replied: 'We must obey God rather than any human authority!'"

Connection

The norm is to obey the authorities; the exception is to resist them. The question that then arises is, "When are we called upon to resist?" Clearly that point comes when obedience to the state entails disobedience to God. There are various examples in Scripture of such "civil disobedience." In Exodus 1:17 the Pharaoh ordered the Hebrew midwives to kill the newborn boys and they refused because they knew this would not please God. In the Book of Daniel King Nebuchadnezzar ordered the people to worship his golden image and the three Hebrew boys refused. Still, it remains difficult to know in every case when government crosses the line and God is opposed so that resistance is called for.

The absolute character of this opening verse is striking to us. There is no room to maneuver. Paul is his most assertive here. "This is the way things are," he says. And indeed this was the case for his readers of this letter. Given their historical circumstances, this was the way of response for them. However, as the discussion in these notes indicates, we need to balance various biblical assertions on this issue against one another. This is a reminder to us that when we study a passage from the Bible our first task is to strive to hear the word of God as those to whom it was first written would have heard it. Then we must apply it carefully to our own circumstances, in the context of the whole of God's revelation.

Verse 2

Context

This being the case, Paul cautions against rebellion. Such rebellion is against what God has instituted and so results in judgment. It is not clear what sort of judgment is in mind: divine judgment or civil judgment. Probably both are in view.

Connection

Three times in these two verses Paul states that the authority of the state comes from God. We have trouble absorbing such a principle knowing from history that the idea of the "divine right" of kings led to massive abuse and that various totalitarian states have claimed God's authority for their human rights violations. Furthermore, there was a time in the near past when there was massive civil disobedience in the United States over such issues as racial integration and the Viet Nam war. Our natural tendency is to be cautious when it comes to ceding great authority to the government. This attitude is further amplified by the more recent sense on the part of some that government is a self-serving, self-perpetuating entity that has lost its vision to serve the people.

So we are left with a dilemma. Paul says that to rebel against authority is to rebel against God. However this assertion (in its historical context) must be weighted against other assertions in the New Testament (in their historical context) with the result that we are called upon to consider carefully the role of government and our response to it. Still, we begin with the sense that properly constituted authority is of God and is to be followed unless to do so is clearly against God's will.

Verse 3

Context

Paul adds a further reason for his statement. It is wise to submit to the governing powers. We have no reason to fear them if we do right because they have been established by God to commend the right and punish the wrong.

Connection

Not all rulers are like this. There have been rulers down through the ages (including Roman rulers) who have turned a blind eye to evil and who have punished the good. What Paul is commending in these verses is the ideal. The "real," when it comes to government, is often far from this "ideal."

Verse 4

Context

Here Paul shifts his theoretical base. In the first three verses he has stated three times that the authority of the state comes from God. Now in these next verses he states that the state has a role given it by God. The word that Paul uses twice to describe the role of the state is *diakonoi* (servant), which is the term he has used elsewhere for ministers of the church. In other words, the state has a ministry and those who perform it (such as judges, police, tax collectors, legislators) are involved in this ministry. Specifically, the ministry of the state is to give approval to those who do good and to punish those who do evil.

"The ruler helps the Christian toward 'the good' which God has in store for him, toward salvation (we take it that it is salvation to which, mainly at any rate 'the good' in the verse refers), if he is a just ruler, by providing him with encouragement to do good and discouragement from doing evil, . . . and by curbing the worst excesses of other men's sinfulness and providing them with selfish reasons for acting justly."[2]

The government has a dual role: to commend the good that is done and to punish the evil that is committed. During Paul's time it was the custom that the state publicly praised those who had done great good and, in fact, rewarded them for it.

Connection

Have you ever thought of public officials as ministers of God? Probably most public officials have not thought of themselves in these terms! And yet they serve God when they uphold the good and inhibit the bad. Certainly this fact is a mandate for Christians to get involved in the running of the state as a God-given ministry. Furthermore, all vocations can be seen as ministries of God when they are performed in such a way so as to serve the purposes of God.

In our day the government seems to confine itself to punishment. Little is done by way of praising those who do good as Paul here understands the role of government to be. "The state tends to be better at punishing than at rewarding, better at enforcing the law than at fostering virtue and service."[3]

Verse 5

Context

Since the Christian knows that God has appointed the ruler, not to obey would create a guilty conscience.

---

2. Cranfield, *Romans*, 666.
3. Stott, *Romans*, 346.

Connection

Most of the time when we break the law we do not feel guilty. We exceed the speed limit, we fudge on taxes, and we cut corners in business. Clearly Paul is challenging such behavior.

Verse 6

Context

Part of the ministry of government is to collect taxes. This would have been a controversial statement on Paul's part given the widespread hostility to taxation in the first century, especially amongst conquered countries and subject peoples. In the first century there were many taxes such as duty, import/export taxes, taxes for the use of roads or for the right to drive a cart, etc.

Connection

Given the complexity of current tax laws, evidence that those with good tax accountants pay less, and the misuse of public tax revenue, we are tempted to be less than strict when it comes to paying taxes. However, Paul is quite clear: pay your taxes. As concerned citizens we probably need to address tax abuses at the level of law not by personal disobedience.

Verse 7

Context

"Revenue" probably refers to the tribute paid by members of subject nations to Rome. This usually consisted of three types of revenue: a general tax on agricultural produce, a 1 percent income tax, and a poll tax paid by everyone between the ages of 14 and 65.

Connection

Paul has something to say here not just about the letter of the law (pay taxes, pay revenue). He also has something to say about the spirit of the law (give respect and honor to public officials).

Session Eleven

Community

The Experience of Change

OVERVIEW

In this session we will examine a case study in which insight, repentance, confession, and faith all come together in quite a dramatic way. This will lead to the whole question of community and the fact that we need others when it comes to the process of change. Our community opens us up to the need for change; our community then helps us to sustain change. The Christian way has always been the way of community.

Unison Prayer

Pray together a prayer by Martin Israel that points to the goal of transformation when it comes to the needs of the world.

> *Let the healing grace of your love, O Lord, so transform us that we may play our part in the transfiguration of the world from a place of suffering, death and corruption to a realm of infinite light, joy and love. Make us so obedient to your Spirit that our lives may become living prayers, and a witness to your unfailing presence. Amen.*[1]

---

1. Appleton, *Oxford Book of Prayer*, 84.

SPIRITUAL TRANSFORMATION

OPEN 20–30 MINUTES

"People, We Need People"

We cannot escape them. We are surrounded by groups of people. We are part of some, we are welcomed by others, we are disliked by still others, and we are not even noticed by most. How do you do when it comes to communities of people?

1. When you were a kid, which events were the most fun for you? Share some memories.

   - ☐ Sunday School picnics
   - ☐ Family picnics
   - ☐ School picnics
   - ☐ Neighborhood picnics
   - ☐ No picnics
   - ☐ Pool parties
   - ☐ Backyard barbeques
   - ☐ Tailgate parties
   - ☐ I hated being outdoors with food and ants (and aunts)

2. Name the various communities of people that made up the neighborhood or area where you grew up? Was this a good, bad, or indifferent experience for you?

3. What is the ideal community of which you would like to be part?

CONSIDER 15–20 MINUTES
An Experience of Transformation

When a decision to change is coupled with faith in God, growth takes place. Rather than theorizing about this any further, let me simply share the experience of a young woman who was a member of a small group that met at our home:

> It was one of our more dramatic small group meetings. Jane (I'll call her) was a fairly new member of the group. Although she had been a Christian for some time, her experience in this area as in most other areas of her life had been stormy. Divorced, living in a small apartment with a job that would soon end, she was lonely, depressed, and suicidal. The group tried, in its small way, to care for Jane.
>
> On the evening in question, Jane had arrived in great spirits. Something had happened and she wanted to tell us about it. We set aside the planned agenda and Jane launched into her story. It seems that she had experienced one of those rare but decisive encounters with God out of which came new and crucial insight into whom she was and what was going on in her life. All alone one evening, she became aware of God's presence and with it a sense that many of her problems could be traced to her failure to take God seriously in one particular area: her sexual life. She knew in a deep and decisive way that she must give up her promiscuity in order to get back on the road to health and wholeness. It was a revelation that made sense to her.
>
> Listening to Jane that evening, we all got the feeling that she was a newly freed woman. She was open, articulate, and happy. She did not feel the need to hide anything. She had faced herself and seen what was really there. And she had accepted this insight from God not as a condemning judgment but as guidance from a loving Parent. She had asked God for forgiveness and felt sure that it had been given. And she had put this destructive pattern of living behind her. The result of all this was that now she had hope.
>
> It struck me than (and we discussed it in the group that evening) that here was a classic (albeit dramatic) example of what repentance and faith is all about. It began with *insight* into the way things really were. Jane had become *aware* of a hitherto unevaluated but destructive pattern of living. Insight had then been followed by a decision to *change*. She decided to stop sleeping around. This change was *made possible* because Jane sensed God's

love for her (not God's condemnation), because she *believed* that God would forgive her if she would but ask, and because the Holy Spirit would assist her in carrying out her intentions.

I was also struck by the result of this act of repentance and faith. By aligning herself with the way she ought to be living, she found new freedom and hope. Repentance and faith had led toward wholeness.[2]

The Nature of Transformation

This is what transformation is all about: confronting an issue, offering it to God by means of repentance and faith, and then moving to a new and better place. What Jane experienced is what we all can and should experience.

Of course, it does not always take place in this way. Mostly transformation is small and simple, not big and dramatic. We do experience times of crises that result in major movement forward (as with Jane). But we also need the unfolding transformation that takes place as we continue to hold our lives open to God on a daily basis.

So we pray regularly and we keep exposing ourselves to Scripture. We worship God and we take time for reflection and meditation. We write in a journal, we join a small group, and we process our stories. And as we do all this we notice things: a relationship that is out of alignment, a hostile reaction to a stranger, too much time spent on activities of too little worth, etc. We offer these to God. We talk about them with others. We investigate Scripture for insight into them. We connect present responses with past experiences so as to get a sense of the psychological dynamic involved. We make choices. We pray and offer these to God in repentance and faith. We leave the issue behind. We take a small step forward. No big deal. We may not even notice what is happening in our lives. It may not even matter if we notice or not because the important thing is our movement in the right direction: toward becoming who we really are in Christ. This is growth. This is discipleship. This is Christian formation.

Thus it is that the process of change becomes part of who we are. This is our aim: to learn the discipline of transformation so that we are open to insight, willing to repent, able to be open with other, and actively reaching out in faith to God—all the time and not just in crises. Growth has become a mindset for us. Growth has become a way of life for us.

---

2. Peace, *Pilgrimage*, 85-86. Other material in this session has been adapted from chapter 8 in *Pilgrimage*.

Community

In all this we need others. It may sound as if we can do it on our own but we cannot. The Christian way has always been the community way. American Christianity may sound, at times, as if all that counts is our personal relationship with Jesus but this is not the biblical view. In Scripture you find community at the heart of God's work in the world. In the Old Testament the most basic reality is the tribe. The tribe gave order and substance to life. In the New Testament the Christian tribe is called the church and it is made up of not just one people but all peoples. It is in the church that growth takes place.

It is hard to read the New Testament without noticing how much space is given to the question of relationships. On one level, this is what the New Testament is all about: relationships—relationship with God, relationship with other Christians, relationship with the surrounding world, relationship with the State. This emphasis on relationships is there because relationships are what the community is all about and the church is, at its heart, a community.

Our growth does not take place outside of relationships, outside of community. In fact, our growth is mostly about getting our relationships in order. We need to grow in loving God and loving others and in the whole process we need to learn to love ourselves properly. It is our relationships with others that both promote growth and sustain growth over time.

Jane needed to tell her small group what had happened. What had happened had been sparked, in part, by what had gone on in the weeks before in her small group. Her growth was affirmed by the group and supported by the group. But we all knew that while the first decision to live in a non-promiscuous way was crucial, Jane would need to reaffirm this decision over and over again. She would need our help with this. On her own she might not be able to make it and she knew it. Without others what had happened to her would only have been an "interesting experience." With the group, this new way of being had the chance to find root in her life. Community is not an added extra to growth; it is at its heart.

What its all about

Transformation is a life-long task. Our goal is to be conformed to the image of Christ: to think as Christ would think, to feel as Christ would feel, and to act as Christ would act. Obviously, we never get this right. We always fall short. Even when we have developed a lifestyle that is as consistent as we can make it in regard to New Testament principles of behavior, our reactions will catch us off guard. We will not always be loving, kind, thoughtful, joy-filled, or honest. We will not always think straight or respond patiently. Furthermore, there is ample testimony from saints far advanced in the Christian way that the more aware one is of God, the more aware one is also aware of personal sin. So we live with the fact that the goal we pursue cannot be reached in this lifetime. But we are also aware that we can and do make progress in becoming conformed to Christ.

I wish that I could say at the end of this book that I write from a place of accomplishment. In fact, I wrestle with all these issues. I get it right sometimes. I have made progress. I do try to be kind and loving. But I have a long ways to go and my childhood issues are far from resolved. But I do know on an ever-deeper level that God loves me. And I do know the power of grace in my life even in the midst of my own failures. I suppose this is a kind of accomplishment. I would like transformation to be magical and complete but I experience it as slow and real and set in the context of pilgrimage—a pilgrimage that will end in the heavenly city when all will be revealed, when death is undone, and where the love of God shines in unfettered radiance that melts away the sin that has so deeply constrained us.

DISCUSSION   10–15 MINUTES

4. Reflect together on Jane's story:

    - What were the various elements that came together to bring about this change in her life?

    - With what part of Jane's story did you resonate most deeply? About which part did you have questions?

    - Had you been at that small group meeting what would you have wanted to say to Jane?

5. Why do we need other people in order to grow?

APPLICATION   10–15 MINUTES

Once again, it might be appropriate to split up into sub-groups of four so that each person has more time to share.

6. Where are you when it comes to growth? Consider such issues as:

   - the name of the problem with which you wrestle
   - the ability to share it with others
   - the willingness to turn from it
   - the ways in which faith is needed
   - the help you need from others
   - the next steps you are being called upon to take

PRAYER   5–10 MINUTES

End this small group session with a time of prayer in which you ask God for:

   - a deep sense of his love as you struggle to grow
   - grace that will enable you to grow
   - a community that will assist and support your growth

REFLECTION   During the week

7. What is your story? Reflect on what you might share with your small group if you could be completely honest. Better still, write this in your journal.

Session Twelve

Love in the Last Days

A Bible Study on Romans 13:8–14

OVERVIEW

What does it mean to live with the expectation that Jesus might return again to this earth in visible form at any moment? How should such an expectation shape our daily lives? These are the questions with which we are left in this final section. However, it is not just questions that are raised here. Paul also provides practical principles that serve to guide us as we make daily choices to live a life of love. And so with this summation he concludes chapters 12 and 13 in which he provides for us his blueprint for how we should live as men and women who seek to follow Jesus.

Unison Prayer

Begin with this contemporary prayer.

> *Lord of Love, help us today to display love in all we think, say, feel, and do. Yet even as we pray this prayer we know that we will fail in this all-consuming task. Only you are perfect love. And so we pray that you will forgive us for our failure to love. But also guide us to become ever better at love and shape us so that we do love. Give us eyes to see others not as rivals or objects to use or people to disdain but as women and men made in your image and loved by you. Enable us to look at others through the eyes of love. We thank you that in calling us to this task of love you transform us so that we are able to love. We pray all this in the name of Jesus who is our model of love. Amen.*

SPIRITUAL TRANSFORMATION

OPEN　　　　　　　　　　　　　　　　　　**20–30 MINUTES**

Saying Good-bye

This is your final session together. Use this *Open* time to reflect on what the whole experience has meant to you. You will have a brief time at the end to consider what to do next as a small group.

1. What have you learned about the nature and process of transformation? Share one insight.

2. How has your study of Romans 12 and 13 shaped your daily life? Share one example.

3. For what are you most grateful in these weeks together as a small group?

THE PASSAGE **5 MINUTES**

Read aloud the following passage in both translations.

Romans 13:8–14

8Owe no one anything, except to love one another; for the one who loves another has fulfilled the law. 9The commandments, "You shall not commit adultery; You shall not murder; You shall not steal; You shall not covet"; and any other commandment, are summed up in this word, "Love your neighbor as yourself." 10Love does no wrong to a neighbor; therefore, love is the fulfilling of the law.

11Besides this, you know what time it is, how it is now the moment for you to wake from sleep. For salvation is nearer to us now than when we became believers; 12the night is far gone, the day is near. Let us then lay aside the works of darkness and put on the armor of light; 13let us live honorably as in the day, not in reveling and drunkenness, not in debauchery and licentiousness, not in quarreling and jealousy. 14Instead, put on the Lord Jesus Christ, and make no provision for the flesh, to gratify its desires. (NRSV)

Don't run up debts, except for the huge debt of love you owe each other. When you love others, you complete what the law has been after all along. The law code–don't sleep with another person's spouse, don't take someone's life, don't take what isn't yours, don't always be wanting what you don't have, and any other "don't" you can think of–finally adds up to this: Love other people as well as you do yourself. You can't go wrong when you love others. When you add up everything in the law code, the sum total is love.

But make sure that you don't get so absorbed and exhausted in taking care of all your day-by-day obligations that you lose track of the time and doze off, oblivious to God. The night is about over, dawn is about to break. Be up and awake to what God is doing! God is putting the finishing touches on the salvation work he began when we first believed. We can't afford to waste a minute, must not squander these precious daylight hours in frivolity and indulgence, in sleeping around and dissipation, in bickering and grabbing everything in sight. Get out of bed and get dressed! Don't loiter and linger, waiting until the very last minute. Dress yourself in Christ, and be up and about! (The Message)

SPIRITUAL TRANSFORMATION

ANALYSIS   15–20 MINUTES

4. What does it mean that we are to owe nothing to anyone except to love?

5. How does love fulfill the law?

6. How does the law (e.g., the Ten Commandments) help you know how to love your neighbor?

7. How does the fact that Jesus is coming back to earth again motivate us to proper living?

APPLICATION   15–20 MINUTES

8. The commandments listed in this passage define what not to do. Take each and make it positive (what to do) in order to understand the way of love:

Law	*Love*
• Do not commit adultery	• Love your spouse warmly
• Do not murder	•
• Do not steal	•
• Do not desire what you don't have	•

9. In what ways is defining love as "not harming others" liberating in how we live?

10. Four principles to guide how we choose to live can be extracted from Paul's discussion:

    - We are to act in love towards all others
    - We are not to harm others
    - We must live in such a way that our acts are open to scrutiny by others
    - We must live as if Jesus could return today

    Discuss how these principles help one to make choices in the following situations:

    - An airport van driver asks you for a tip even though he has been rude and you were uncomfortable since he had overfilled the van.
    - You are married and yet you find a co-worker to be particularly attractive.
    - Your neighbor has an unruly child.

11. End this section by reading aloud again *The Message* paraphrase of this passage.

FAREWELL   10–20 MINUTES

12. What is the next step for you as a small group?

    ❐ Study together another book in the *Spiritual Disciplines* series

    ❐ Continue this group and do the studies you missed (if any) in this book

    ❐ Continue this as a covenant group in which you assist one another in the practice of various spiritual disciplines

    ❐ Start new small groups in which to work with others on the process of transformation

    ❐ Disband as a group but have a reunion meal in a month

    ❐ Say good-bye and join a new group

13. In your final prayer together, focus on the Romans 13:11–12 (from *The Message*). With your eyes closed and minds focused on God, listen as your leader reads aloud the passage below twice. As he or she reads, listen for the words or phrase from this selection that resonates with you. In the silence that follows, meditate on those words or phrase. What is God saying to you? How do these words or phrase connect with your life? When the silent meditation ends, join in prayer together offering back to God what you have been thinking and feeling in your meditation. Also offer one another to God in prayer, thanking God for each other and for these weeks together in the small group.

The night is about over, dawn is about to break. Be up and awake to what God is doing! God is putting the finishing touches on the salvation work he began when we first believed. We can't afford to waste a minute, must not squander these precious daylight hours . . .

BIBLE STUDY NOTES
Overview

Paul moves from specific instructions on relationships (e.g., "do not take revenge" 12:14) to the general principle that guides all relationships: the law of love (13:8–10). He has three things to say: 1) love is a debt ("owe no one anything") which we can never fully repay, 2) love is the fulfillment of God's law, and 3) love does not harm (wrong) others. He then ends this long unit which began in chapter 12 by pointing out what it is that motivates Christians to follow this law of love, namely the expectation of the imminent return of Christ. Paul's summary of the Christian life in 13:8–14 is therefore: "Love others because the new age is dawning."

Verse 8

Context

Paul uses the concept of "debt" or "owing someone" to make a transition from the Christian's responsibility to the state to the Christian's responsibility to others. We are called to pay promptly all our bills and taxes but there is one debt that we can never completely pay: the debt of love. We can never say, "I have loved to the full. I do not need to love more." The Church Father, Origen, put it this way: "So Paul desires that our debt of love should remain and never cease to be owed; for it is expedient that we should both pay all this debt daily and always owe it."[1]

Paul then goes on to make a second assertion: when we love others we fulfill the law. This is an amazing assertion for a man who had, prior to his conversion, spent enormous energy seeking to keep the law (he was a Pharisee). It is love, empowered by the Holy Spirit, that enables us to live the way God wishes us to live. Notice too that the emphasis is on loving all people, not just those in the Christian community as the phrase "love one another" implies.

Connection

Law and love are sometimes seen as incompatible. Law is pictured as being harsh and demanding in contrast to love that takes into account the person. Law is negative ("thou shalt not") whereas love is positive ("do unto others"). But this is not a fully accurate contrast. For one thing, the law can be generous (as when rules for the care of the poor are prescribed) and love can be hard (as when love says "No" to the wrongly directed desires of another). For another thing, "love and law need each other. Love needs law for its direction, while law needs love for its inspiration."[2] We need to remember this fact in our cultural environment in which morality has become subjective ("Do what you want as long as no one gets hurt") and compassion has lost its shape ("Love is whatever I give you after I have what I want"). Without a sense of the character of love (which law provides) we are apt to name certain actions and attitudes as "love" when, in fact, they do not deserve that name. Augustine put law and love together in an interesting fashion when he said, "Love God—and do what you like." What he means is that if you truly love God, your life will automatically fall into those patterns established by the written law. What you will like when you love God is what God wishes for us. Still, since all people are sinful and therefore imperfect, the admonitions of the Ten Commandments as well as those of St. Paul will be of great value by helping to clarify the path of love.

Verse 9

Context

Paul points to the second half of the Ten Commandments and indicates that each law would be automatically fulfilled if people kept the more basic

1. Cranfield, *Romans*, 674.
2. Stott, *Romans*, 350.

principle that underlies them—loving others in the same fashion in which they love themselves. If a person really loved his neighbor, he wouldn't steal from him, etc.

Connection

The gauge by which we know that we indeed love others is proper self-love. Proper self-love, however, is very difficult to get right in contemporary culture that pushes us to an inflated self-esteem. Our goal as Christians is to know ourselves fully and accurately ("think of yourself with sober judgment" as Paul tells us in 12:3) and to value ourselves as God values us (God loves us) so we do not fall into either too inflated or too depressed a view of ourselves. We need to know who we are as men and women in Christ. Then we can seek to love others in ways we would want to be loved and we would have some sense that our actions toward other are most likely loving since they accord with how we would want to be treated.

Verse 10

Context

Paul now states the negative side of what he has just said. Loving your neighbor means not "harming" him or her (as the NIV translates "wronging"). Breaking the commandments that Paul has named harms people. In contrast, love has as its goal the good of our neighbor. This is how love fulfills the law.

Connection

The call not to harm others may, at first, seem weak. Instead of putting this in the negative ("do not harm") why not put it in the positive ("seek the highest good of others")? In fact, we already know this is the way we should live. This is what the so-called golden rule tells us, "Do to others what you would have them do to you" (Matt 7:12). However, the call not to harm gives us a new slant on love. Loving others can be very difficult at times. But at least we can make sure that we do not harm others and know that this is an act of love. We can act this way even to our enemies (remember that Paul has just been discussing enemies). Not harming is a good beginning. Hopefully it will lead to more positive acts.

Verse 11

Context

Paul now moves to conclude chapters 12 and 13. He does so by reminding his readers that the present dark-age is drawing to a close and the kingdom of God is dawning. In such an environment they are to live as citizens of God's kingdom and not as citizens of the dark kingdom. In other words, Paul is giving them (and us) the motivation to live in the ways he has outlined in these two chapters. The idea of the Second Coming as that which motivates one to live morally can also be found elsewhere in the New Testament (see Matt 25:31–46; Mark 13:32–37; Phil 4:4–7; 1 Thess 5:1–11, 23; Heb 10:24–25; Jam 5:4–11; and 1 Pet 4:7–11).

Paul understands that the present age within which believers now live is not the ultimate reality. It is merely the prelude to a greater reality that will burst forth when Christ returns again to earth. The early church understood that the life, death, and resurrection of Jesus had ushered in the last days—the end time. God, however, because of God's patience has provided an *interval* before the culmination of the "night," the purpose of which is to allow other men and women to come to faith. During this interval the call to the Christian is to remain alert and expectant knowing that the Second Coming may occur at any time. Therefore Christians are not to live as if the here and now is all there is. Rather, remembering what Christ did in the past, they are to set their eyes on the future and live a life-style consistent with the coming new age. This is how the Second Coming motivates one to moral living. Here salvation is understood as a divine event that will take place at a particular time in the future, i.e., though one enters into salvation upon conversion, this is a state to be realized fully only at the Second Coming.

Connection

Are we really motivated by the sense that Christ may return at any moment so that we need to have our house in order and our life under control? I think not. After all, or so we reason, it has been 2000 years and Jesus still has not returned. So we say, "Chances are that he will not return in my lifetime either." But this misses the point. Christ is already present for us as he has been for all his followers at all times. His physical return will simply be the visible manifestation of this fact. This is what we pray when we say the Lord's Prayer, "Thy kingdom come, on earth as it is in heaven." Thus we

Spiritual Transformation

need to live always with the sense that just as Jesus came once, is here now, so he will come again. Time makes no difference. Jesus is present and so we live in a way that is consistent with this reality.

Verse 12

Context

The "night" is the old age in which darkness prevailed. The "day" is the time when Christ returns again. Our attitude should be that Jesus' return can happen at any moment. The date does not matter. We are always to be in a state of readiness. This being the case we are to put off our night clothes ("works of darkness") and put on instead what soldiers of Christ are called to wear ("the armor of light" as in Eph 6:11–17).

Connection

We understand intuitively the difference between works of darkness and works of light. That which is done in the dark is hidden, secretive, and shameful. Were it to be brought into the light it would be exposed for what it really is. It could not stand the scrutiny of light. This is why Christians are called to "walk in the light" (1 John 1:5–2:2) so that what we do can stand whatever scrutiny might be brought to bear. This principle gives us a powerful way to assess any deed we might contemplate: Can it stand the light? Can we do this thing in clear view of anyone (especially those that it impacts) or must it be hidden? If the deed cannot stand the light then it is not to be done.

Verse 13

Context

Here Paul defines for us the works of darkness. He names various dark deeds. Each focuses on the lack of self-control in the areas of drink, sex, and social relationships.[3]

Connection

Just as Paul has called us to a quite specific life style (which he has defined in the previous sections), so now he points to the kind of life style we are to flee. The issues he names sound strangely familiar. What was true in first century Rome is still true in twenty-first century America. Deeds of

---

3. Stott, *Romans*, 353.

darkness are still deeds of darkness. We are still afflicted by various sexual temptations, alcoholism and drug addiction are a very real issue, and tense relationships characterize our culture. Thus Paul's call to leave all this behind is as fresh as when he first gave it nearly two thousand years ago.

Verse 14:

Context

To put on the armor of light (v. 12) is, in fact, to put on Christ. It is not merely a matter of cultivating Christian virtues independently, on one's own. "To put on the Lord Jesus Christ means here to embrace again and again, in faith and confidence, in grateful loyalty and obedience, Him to whom we clearly belong. It means to follow Him in the way of discipleship and to strive to let our lives be molded according to the pattern of the humility of His earthly life. It means so trusting in Him and relying wholly upon the state of righteousness before God which is ours in Him, that we cannot help but live to please Him."[4]

Connection

In the summer of A.D. 386, Aurelius Augustine, Professor of Rhetoric at Milan University sat weeping in a friend's garden, wanting to begin a new life but not knowing how, when he heard a child chanting, "Take Up and Read! Take Up and Read!" Whereupon he picked up his friend's copy of Romans and read Romans 13:13-14. "No further could I read," he later wrote, "nor had I any need; instantly, at the end of the sentence, a clear light flooded my heart and all the darkness of doubt vanished away."[5]

Summary

So, then, what are the essential features of the life to which we have been called as followers of Jesus? In other words, what is the goal of transformation? What are we to become as we seek to be conformed to the image of Christ? In what direction does our on-going change move? These are all ways of asking the same foundational question.

Paul has begun to give us an answer to this question in Romans 12 and 13. (The whole of the New Testament must be consulted for the full answer,

---

4 Cranfield, *Romans*, 688–689.
5. Augustine, *Confessions*, 153.

however.) In summary, here is what Paul in his role as an apostle of Jesus urges us to do.

In Romans 12 and 13 Paul defines what our relationships should look like in seven different directions:

- To God (12:1–2)
- To ourselves (12:3–8)
- To others (12:9–16)
- To our enemies (12:17–21)
- To the state (13:1–7)
- To the law (13:8–10)
- To the day of the Lord's return (13:11–14)

In this way, he provides for us a coherent map for what the transformed life ought to look like. Clearly no one has got it right in each of these areas. Growth is connected to our progress in getting it right in each of these areas.

In summary he is saying:

- *Transformation is normative.* Transformation must become a mindset, a way of life for us. The direction in which transformation moves is clearly defined. Our aim is to follow "God's will." However, we will be pulled in the opposite direction, toward the ways of the world. But our call is to resist being conformed to "the pattern of the world." The basic dynamic for transformation is defined: it is renewal of our minds (Romans 12:1–2).

- *The primary environment of growth is the community of Christ's people.* We need to understand the nature of that community. There is a foundational unity that binds everyone together regardless of race, gender, position in life, etc. None of these human differences matter. The essential reality that creates the community is the fact that all are "one in Christ." But each person has a different and essential role to play in order for the whole community to be healthy. Our task is to discern our spiritual gifts and use them for the sake of others.

- *Relationships within the community of Christ must revolve around love.* And the love to which Paul refers is not some ill-defined feeling of general benevolence toward others. It has quite specific characteristics, which are seen in how we think about others, feel about others, and act toward others. These characteristics include sincerity, discernment, affection, honor, enthusiasm, joy-filled patience and faithfulness, generosity, hospitality, good will, solidarity, harmony, and humility. Much of the transformation we will see in ourselves over time will have to do with learning the ways of love.

- *When it comes to our relationships with those who persecute us and treat us as enemies, we owe the same debt of love to them.* We are not to retaliate, curse, or take revenge on enemies. Instead we are to serve them by blessing them, doing what is right, living at peace with them as far as we are able, and overcoming evil with good. We leave it to God to deal with evil.

- *When it comes to the State our basic stance is that its authority comes from God.* We are to submit to that authority, pay our taxes, and give honor to those who are agents of the state, because theirs is a ministry. But when the state ceases to restrain evil and reward good, then we must consider whether we must "obey God rather than man."

- *In the end it all comes down to love.* The commandments (law) give shape to love; love fulfills the demands of this law. Love is very practical. If it means nothing else it means not harming others. Our motivation to live a life of love is that this is the way of the new age that is dawning. Jesus is coming again so we must shed deeds of darkness and give ourselves to the way of light, which is the way of Christ. To be transformed is to take on the clothing of Jesus Christ.

Leader's Notes for This Study

Starting a Spiritual Transformation Small Group

All it takes to start a group is the willingness of one person to make some phone calls. When you invite people to consider joining the small group, be sure to explain how the group will operate since this is a different sort of small group. See "How to Use this Guide" at the front of the book which explains the nature of the group.

The best way to use this material is to do each session in order. However, this will involve twelve sessions. If your group does not have that much time there are various options you can choose:

- *Work through a reduced number of chapters.* Simply select the sessions that interest you most, doing as many sessions as your schedule allows. Do the sessions in order since they build on one another. If you skip a session, have each person read through the missed chapter on his or her own.

- *Do only the sessions on the process of transformation.* These are the odd numbered sessions.

- *Do only the Bible studies on Romans 12 & 13.* These are the even numbered sessions.

Find a comfortable place to meet, preferably in a home with a room in which you circle the chairs so everyone can see the eyes of the others (which is prerequisite for a group conversation). Make plans to deal with potential distractions such as children, pets, and cell phones.

Get enough copies of the books so each person has one. The book contains all the information needed for each of the small group sessions.

Leader's Notes for This Study

The Art of Small Group Leadership

It is not difficult to be a small group leader. All you need is:

- The willingness to do so.
- The commitment to read through all the materials prior to the session (including the leader's notes for that session).
- The sensitivity to others that will allow you to guide the discussion without dominating it.
- The willingness to be used by God as a small group leader.

Here are some basic small group principles that will help you do your job.

Ask the questions:

Just read the questions and let various group members respond.

Guide the discussion:

Ask follow-up questions (or make comments) that draw others into the discussion and keeps the discussion going. For example: "John, how would you answer the question?" or "Anybody else have any insights into this question?" or "Let's move on to the next question."

Start and stop on time:

Your job is to start the group on time and, most importantly, to stop it on time. Certain people will always be late so don't wait until they arrive. Most importantly, end on time. If you don't people will be hesitant to come again since they never know when they will get home.

Stick to the time allotted to each section:

There is always more that can be said in response to any question. So, if you do not stick carefully to the time limits for each section you will never finish the study. And this usually means the group will miss out on the really important application questions at the end of the session. It is your job to make sure that the discussion keeps moving from question to question. This means you may have to keep saying, "Well, it is time to move on to the next question." You may not be able to ask all the questions. Know the material well enough so that you can select the most important questions and skip the rest. Remember: it is better to cut off discussion when it is going well than to let it go on until it dies out.

Model answers to questions:

Whenever you ask a question to which everyone is expected to respond (for example, an Open question as opposed to an Analysis question), you, as leader, should be the first person to respond. In this way you model the right length of response. If you take 5 minutes to respond, everyone else in the group will feel that it is okay for them to take at least 5 minutes (so just one question might take 50 minutes for the whole group of ten to answer!). But if you take one minute to answer so will everyone else (and the question takes only 10 minutes for the group to answer). Also, by responding first, you model an appropriate level of openness. Remember, the leader should be a bit more vulnerable than others.

Understand the intention of different kinds of questions:

You will ask the group various kinds of questions. It is important for you to understand the purpose of each kind of question:

- *Experience questions*: These are often the first type of question you will ask. The aim of these questions is to get people to recall past experiences and share these memories with the group. There is no right or wrong answer to these questions. Such questions facilitate the group process by getting people to share their stories with one another, by being easy to answer so everyone has something to say and thus the group conversation begins, or by getting people to think about the session topic on the basis of their own experience.

- *Forced-choice questions*: Certain questions will be followed by a series of suggested answers (with check-boxes next to each possible answer). Generally no one answer is correct. In fact, often each answer is correct! By offering options, group members are aided in responding. This also helps direct the response. When people answer such questions, you may want to ask them to explain why they chose the answer they did.

- *Analysis or Discussion questions*: These are questions that force the group to notice what the biblical text or Consider material says and to probe it for meaning.

- *Application questions*: These questions seek to help the group make connections between the meaning of the text and each person's life circumstance.

Leader's Notes for This Study

- *Questions with multiple parts*: Sometimes a question is asked and then various aspects of it are listed below. Have the group seek to answer each of the sub-questions. Their answers, taken together, will answer the initial question.

Introduce each section:

This may involve a brief overview of the focus, purpose, or topic of the section plus instructions on how to do the exercise.

Comments:

Occasionally it will be helpful to the group if you bring into the discussion some useful information that you have gotten from your own study. Never make long comments. Do not allow yourself to become the "expert" to whom everyone turns for "the right answer." Invite comments from others.

Notes on Each Session

Prior to each session, go over the notes for that particular session. These focus on the specific materials in the session. The assumption in this book is that virtually anyone can lead a small group session since all the necessary material is contained in this book. However, when a small group leader has an understanding of the background and goal of each part of the small group experience, he or she is better able to lead. This is the intention of these notes: to provide background material for each session. This section is not the place where the "answers" to the small group questions are given. Most good small group questions do not have a single right answer. They are meant to provoke discussion and sharing that will bring together the collective wisdom of the group. Nor does this section contain "secrets" to which only the leader has access. In fact, group members will be better equipped to participate in the sessions if they take the time to read these notes for leaders.

These notes are "front-loaded." By that I mean there are far more notes for session 1 than for session 12. The general comments about the various parts of the first two sessions apply to all the other sessions so there is no need to repeat them. Thus in subsequent sessions, only that information specific to that session is given.

There are two times indicated for each section. The first is for groups that meet for sixty minutes; the second for groups that meet for ninety minutes. Follow these guidelines carefully. Otherwise you will not have time for the final section of the small group session.

At the end of each session is a section entitled "Reflection." The purpose of this section is to identify one or more questions for consideration by each group member during the week between each small group session. Reflection on these questions will deepen and personalize the material that has been discussed together. While it is possible to meditate on these questions while walking, driving, or just sitting quietly, it is best to write your responses in a journal. A journal is a powerful tool for spiritual growth.[1]

Session One: The Process of Transformation

Preparation: Get enough copies of this book so that each person has his or her own. The book contains all the information needed for each of the small group sessions.

The Special Character of Session One:

The first session is most important. During this session some of those attending will be deciding whether they want to be a part of the group. So your aim as small group leader is to:

- Create excitement about this particular small group (so that each person will want to continue in the group).
- Give people an overview of the whole series (so they will know where the group is headed).
- Begin to build relationships (so that a sense of community starts to develop).
- Encourage commitment to being a part of the small group (so that everyone will return next week, bringing along a friend if possible!).

A good way to launch the first session of any small group is by eating together prior to the session. Sharing a meal draws people together and breaks down barriers between them. Ask everyone to bring along one dish for the supper. This makes it easy to have a meal for 12! Or, if you feel ambitious, you might want to invite everyone to dinner at your place. What you serve need not be elaborate. Conversation not feasting is the intention of

---

1. See Peace, *Spiritual Journaling*.

the get-together. The aim of the meal is to get to know one another in this informal setting. Structure the meal in such a way that a lot of conversation takes place. Following the meal, be sure to do the first session in a complete and full form (and not just talk about what you are going to do when the group starts). Your aim is to give everyone the experience of what it would mean to be a part of this small group.

The odd-numbered sessions consist of the examination of the dynamics of transformation. The comments that follow will apply, in general terms, to all six of these sessions.

Overview:

The role of the overview section is to provide a road map for the group through the material for each particular session. Small groups work better when everyone is informed about where the group is going and what steps will be taken to get there. The more the group knows about what they will be doing together and why, the better they are able to participate. Begin each new small group session with a quick look at the Overview.

Introduction/Overview of Series:

Begin by welcoming each person to the group. Explain the overall purpose of this small group series using the *How to Use this Guide* section. It is not necessary to go over each point. People can read this section on their own. Just make sure they understand:

- *The purpose of the series*: to come to understand how Christian transformation takes place so as to develop a lifestyle that is open always to growth and change. You can point out the types of issues that will be covered by looking together at the Contents page.
- *The details of the session*: when, where, and for how long you will meet.
- *The expectations for each group member*: full participation, appropriate honesty, and regular attendance. (These details will be discussed more fully in Session Two when you go over the Small Group Covenant together.)
- *Make sure the group understands the purpose of the first session*: to discuss the dynamics of transformation so as to have an overview of where the small group is headed.

Leader's Notes for This Study

- *End the Introduction/Overview by leading the group in the unison prayer found in the Overview.* In each session there will be some sort of prayer with which to begin. You may also want to add prayer of your own following the unison prayer. In subsequent sessions you may wish to ask certain group members to pray following the unison prayer or you may wish to open the time to spontaneous group prayer.

Open:

The aim of this exercise is two-fold: to begin the process of getting to know one another and to begin to think about each person's experience of transforming moments, albeit in a lighthearted fashion. This is characteristic of Open exercises: they encourage sharing, they are playful rather than heavy (the heavy discussion comes towards the end of the small group session), and they often provoke humorous responses.

- *Question 1*: This is a way of introducing yourselves to one another. Warning: Unless you watch carefully, each person will take far too long giving these details. As leader you begin by answering this question yourself. Take no more than 60 to 90 seconds for your response. Go around the circle, beginning with you as leader, and give each person time to share. This is called a circle response.

- *Question 2*: Transforming moments are not all big, awesome events. Mostly they are small and incidental but they are nonetheless important. These "examples" are mostly lighthearted but still, a kid leaves behind something of his/her childhood with the discovery of the true nature of Santa. There are other discoveries of this sort in childhood that are more serious (e.g., the discovery that your parents are getting divorced) but stay with non-traumatic issues during his exercise.

- *Question 3*: This allows each person to declare some of his/her agenda for the small group.

Time:

Watch the time carefully. It is very easy to spend more than the allotted 20 to 30 minutes since it is such fun sharing stories. However, be sure to end on time. Otherwise you will not get though the rest of the material, which

Leader's Notes for This Study

is the heart of the session. Remember that the important thing is not "getting through all the questions" in the Open module. The important thing is inviting each person to speak. End this module on time even if you have not covered all the questions.

Consider:

This is the point at which information is provided for the small group about the topic under consideration. It is important that each group member has some grasp of this material since it provides the basis for the subsequent small group sharing. There are different ways to access this information:

- *Homework*: Each person agrees to read over the material prior to the small group session. This is the best option since it takes up the least amount of small group time. During the group session, when you come to this point, allow people a couple of minutes to review the material again before launching into the Discussion and Application exercises. Also, adjust the time available for these two exercises since you will not need all of the 15 to 20 minutes allocated to the Consider section.

- *Silent Reading*: Give people time to read through this section on their own at this point in the small group session. This will not take 15 to 20 minutes. Use the remaining time in the Consider section to highlight key points for the group (what is the essence of each sub-unit of the material?) or to ask: "What is not clear to you?" However, remember that in the Discussion section you will be processing this material.

- *Presentation*: As small group leader, go over the material with the group. Identify the main points of each sub-section. Point out key sentences. Read small excerpts aloud. In other words, use the available time to make an oral presentation of the printed material. It is not necessary to research the subject and present materials beyond what is in the study guide. Just make sure people understand what is provided. You might wish to ask a different person to do this each week.

- *Oral Reading*: This is the most time consuming (and probably most boring) way of presenting the material. Ask different people to read aloud different sections. Still, it may be the best method for your particular group.

Discussion:

Sometimes the discussion will focus on the details of the material in the Consider section. At other times it will ask people to look for experiences in their own lives that illustrate what the text has said. Often, there will be a mixture of questions. In a session such as this one where the majority of the questions focus on group experience not the text, you might want to precede this sharing with questions that make sure the group has understood the Consider material. General questions can be used such as: "Is anything not clear to you?" "What do you think the main point is in the section on The Goal of Transformation (or some other section)?" "How would you summarize what is being said?" "What new things did you learn from this material"?

- *Question 4*: The aim of this question is to make concrete what sudden transforming moments are like in real life. Not everyone in the group will necessarily have had such an experience but some will. Remember, no more than 15 to 20 percent of people have sudden conversion experiences. Most come to faith gradually. Notice that questions 4–6 are "forced choice" questions that provide a series of possible responses. This sort of question is good for getting everyone involved in the conversation.

- *Question 5*: This is an agenda-setting question; a way for group members to declare the kinds of things they would like to see changed in their own lives. This is one way of defining the arena in which each person's work will be centered during the life of this small group.

- *Question 6*: This moves the discussion from sudden transformation to other kinds of transformation. It also assumes that all people are involved in the transforming process in some way.

- *Question 7*: This is an example of a discussion question that focuses on the details of the Consider material.

Application:

The difference between the Discussion section and the Application section is that Discussion focuses on the ideas in the Consider section while Application focuses on the group members and how these ideas might be applied.

- *Question 8*: This is a "dreaming" or "what if" kind of question in which the group is invited to move from *what is* to *what might be*. These kinds of questions serve to open up new possibilities.
- *Question 10*: This question uses a case study as its basis. This case contains all five of the points in the outline of the transformational process and will help people make that process real in their minds. The issue chosen as an illustration is intentionally not an issue of "spiritual change" (though it could be argued that our health is, in fact, a spiritual issue since it is God who gave us bodies and charged us with keeping them in good running order and using them for the kingdom's sake). The point is that the dynamics of change remain constant regardless of the area of concern.

Prayer:

In each of the odd-numbered sessions you will end with free-form prayer that focuses on the issues discussed. How you pray together will depend on the group, its experience in public prayer, and its comfort-level when it comes to praying out-loud. As leader, take charge of the prayer session. Model the kind of prayer you hope for. Model openness in prayer. Here are some points to consider:

- *Make the prayer conversational.* Although the ancient prayers use Thee and Thou you don't have to do that. Talk to God as you would talk to a friend.
- *Make each prayer short and to the point.* There is a habit amongst some people to begin praying and then go one for 5 or 10 minutes during which he/she prays about a host of issues. While there are settings in which this is appropriate, this is not one of them. For one thing, you do not have enough time. For another, you want to draw everyone into prayer. So each person should focus on one topic only and pray no more than 2 or 3 sentences. You can always pray a second or third time.
- *Make the prayer personal.* You will notice that the topics suggested for prayer all relate to the needs of the individual group member. Pray for yourself as others join in by way of affirmation.

Leader's Notes for This Study

- For those who have little experience in public prayer you might want to *give time at the start to let people write out prayers* (or notes) if they wish.

Reflection:

This provides one way by which the impact of the group lives on during the week between sessions. The questions invite mulling over, in a personal way, key issues that were raised during the group discussion. The best way to do this is by journaling your thoughts.

Session Two: The Renewing of Our Minds (Romans 12:1–2)

The even-numbered sessions consist of Bible studies focused on passages from Romans 12 and 13. The comments that follow will apply, in general terms, to all six of these sessions.

Unison Prayer:

As it so happens in this case the second unison prayer is also from St. Anselm. The opening prayer in each of the twelve sessions is a written prayer, generally drawn from ancient sources. As such, they remind us that down through the ages there have been countless men and women who have had the same deep desire to know and follow God. Such prayers also serve a second purpose. They enrich our own prayer vocabularies as we learn from the piety and wisdom of ages past.

Open:

This will be a different sort of Open discussion in that it looks at the question of a small group covenant and not at the experience of group members. It is an important session because a group covenant binds a group together.

Text:

Read aloud both translations of the passage. You can do this as leader or ask someone else to do it. Do not ask someone to read a passage aloud without having first asked them, privately, if they would be willing to do so. The ability to read printed material varies even amongst adults. Be sure to keep the two translations in their proper places. The NRSV version is the study version. It is close to the Greek and so better able to catch Paul's nuances.

Leader's Notes for This Study

The Message is a more free-form translation that seeks to render the passage into words modern people will understand. It will be of great use in the Application process.

Analysis:

The aim of this section of the discussion is to examine the text in such a way that small group members will notice what is there and come to understand its meaning. The questions are of two sorts: observation questions that force people to notice the text and interpretation questions that help them to understand the text. Observation questions do not lend themselves to discussion since it is merely a matter of stating what is noticed (and thus helping one another to see what is there). Interpretation questions create more discussion since they require reflection and synthesis of observations.

You are limited in the time allocated to this section. You will often be pressed for time, however, do not go over the time limit or you will not get to the rest of the study. You may need to drop some questions or combine questions to stay in the time frame.

- *Question 5*: This is an observation question. It is important because it unlocks the structure of the passage: three imperatives that define the process of transformation. Be alert to the fact that some people may be unaware of the term "imperative verb." You might rephrase the question and ask people to identify the main action words in the passage.

- *Question 6*: This is an interpretation question in that the answer is not drawn directly from the text itself and so it requires reflection. Furthermore, there is not a single "right" answer. Here is where the Bible Study Notes will be of use. You might want to give people time to reflect on the questions in this section and to consult the Bible Study Notes before you begin the discussion. You, as leader, ought to have read the Bible Study Notes with some care so as to better guide the discussion. The Bible Study Notes do not give the "answers" to the discussion questions as much as provide background information on each verse.

Application:

The aim of this section is to make connections between what the group has come to understand the passage to mean and the life issues of each person.

Leader's Notes for This Study

Scripture is not meant simply to be understood (though that is crucial), it is meant to be lived out. A small group is a powerful vehicle for helping individuals to grasp the personal significance of a text and then apply it to their lives.

Again, be sensitive to time. You can easily take far more time on this section than is allocated. If time becomes a problem for your group, you might want to break up into sub-groups of four to go over the Application questions. This will give individuals more time to talk, share, and reflect together. Come back together as a whole group for the final prayer exercise. (Make sure that the sub-groups of four contain different group members each week so they do not become mini-groups within the larger group.)

- *Question 9*: This question focuses on the application of the first imperative: *presenting our bodies to God*.

- *Questions 10 & 11*: These two questions focus on the application of the second imperative: *not conforming to the pattern of the world*.

- *Question 12*: This question focuses on the application of the third imperative: *being transformed*. It helps sum up the direction of the passage as a whole and its application to each person.

- *Question 13*: This question, or a variation of it, will be asked at the end of each Bible study. It seeks to keep the focus on the purpose of these Bible studies, which is to define the nature of the transformed life. Group members are invited to use Paul's assertions as a way of examining their own lives and so gaining insight into the direction their growth should take. Be sure not to skip this question.

- *Question 14*: If you have time, re-read *The Message* version of the passage. It will make much better sense now.

Bible Study Notes:

These can be used by the group during the session itself or read individually afterwards. As small group leader you need to go over these notes several times. They will help you guide the discussion. You may want to refer people to certain notes. The notes are structured as follows:

- *Overview*: This gives background information for the whole passage.
- *Context*: This gives background information for the verse or verses.

Leader's Notes for This Study

- *Connection*: This is a reflection on the application of the verse to our individual situations.

If you do not use the Bible Study Notes during the small group discussion, assign them as homework. Suggest that people continue to mull over the passage, assisted by the Bible Study Notes. Suggest that they reflect on whether the connections suggested relate to their own lives.

Prayer:

End the session with a time of meditative prayer. Your task as leader is to:

- Give a brief introduction to this type of prayer. Describe the process: after a brief relaxation exercise you as leader will read the passage twice as they listen for those words or phrases that touch their hearts and draw them to God. There will be a short time for silent reflection (two to three minutes), after which the group members are invited to pray briefly, based on their reflections.
- After this explanation, invite the group to quiet their hearts and minds and to open themselves to the Word of God.
- As they sit in silence, with eyes closed, read slowly the selection from Romans. Pause. Read it a second time.
- Invite people to meditate in silence (two to three minutes).
- You as leader should break the silence by offering a brief model prayer based on your own reflection.
- After all who wish to pray have had the opportunity, end the prayer time with a short prayer of conclusion.
- If you have time, discuss together this experience of meditative prayer.[2]

Session Three: Insight

Open:

All three questions are of the "forced choice" variety. The point is not simply to indicate your "choice" but to tell the group the reason for your selection.

---

2. This form of prayer, *lectio divina*, is described more fully in Peace, *Contemplative Bible Reading*, which is part of the *Spiritual Disciplines Study Guide* series.

Leader's Notes for This Study

Tell a story that illustrates your choice. The point is not so much to answer these blindly as it is to use the question to stimulate sharing. Forced choice questions also serve the function of stretching our understanding of certain issues simply by looking over the range of possible choices.

Consider:

This should be an easier set of material to comprehend (as compared to the first session) because it focuses on one thing only: the various ways in which insight comes into our lives.

Discussion:

The aim in the discussion is to make real the various kinds of input that bring about change by illustrating them from the lives of the small group members.

Session Four: Knowing Ourselves (Romans 12:3–8)

As you move into your second Bible study, remember why it is you are studying Romans 12 & 13 and how these chapters connect with the central theme of transformation. Knowing this will enable you to keep the focus sharp in the Bible study. The Bible is so rich in what it says that it is possible for a group to get off on tangents by looking at other themes in the passage. Don't let this happen!

Open:

- *Question 3*: The aim is not to "brag" but it is to claim our successes. Christians sometimes have a hard time accepting success. We are much better at admitting failure! But we all have gifts (which is the point of this session) and if we don't claim them we can't thank God for them or use them for God's glory.

Analysis:

Questions 4–6a are Fact questions and can be answered quickly by reference to the passage. Discussion will be generated via questions 6b–7.

Prayer:

Follow the instructions in the Leader's Notes for Session Two.

Session Five: Repentance

Open:

The aim is not so much to share "deep, dark secrets" as it is to remember and share the funny little incidents of growing up (though they may have been traumatic at the time). The point is that we all have a history of not always doing it right.

Application:

You shift into a new form of discussion and sharing in this small group session. You will have been together for five weeks. Hopefully, a certain amount of trust will have developed between group members. Now you are being asked to move from discussion of change in general terms to discussion of change in personal terms. In sessions five, seven, nine, and eleven people are given the opportunity to work on real issues of personal growth. The small group is the ideal environment in which to do this work. Thus the directions in this section become more general. You may just want to give people opportunity to talk about what it is they are wrestling with. Potentially, this can be the most significant part of the whole small group experience.

You might want to break up into sub-groups of four each. In this way each person has more time in which to share. Be sure to come back together as a whole group for the final time of prayer.

The way to handle the discussion in session five is to examine, in turn, each of the areas listed. Not everyone will have something to say in each area. In fact, you may need to say "Given our limited time, pick one of these areas in which to share." Remember that as leader you play a crucial role. It will be up to you to begin the personal sharing and your openness will set the tone for openness on the part of others.

Session Six: Loving Others (Romans 12:9–16)

See the discussion under Session Two for information about how this type of session is to function.

Open:

- *Question 1:* It will be interesting to hear the variety of groups with which people have been associated. Be sure to include not just

Leader's Notes for This Study

churches but para-church groups as well as other communities (such as Retreat Centers).

Analysis:

Rather than a series of questions, in this case there is one major question with twelve parts that should occupy most of your time as well as helping people to see the inter-connections within the passage. Use question 5 as a summary question if you have time.

Application:

Again, the focus is on a few questions rather than many questions. You could put the weight of your discussion on either question 6 or 7. Do not neglect question 8 which is the common question in each of the Bible studies that seeks to define the nature of the transformed life.

Prayer:

The focus of the meditation is on six of the sayings from Romans 12:9–16. When this meditation exercise is completed, if there is time, you might want to discuss this way of accessing the meaning of the text. Has this been a valuable exercise for the group?

Session Seven: Confession

See the discussion under Session One for information about how this type of session is to function.

Open:

The most important question is number three in which you affirm one another. This is a valuable group building exercise so do not skip it.

Application:

 Continue the process of personal sharing around issues of important for each individual.

Session Eight: Service not Retaliation (Romans 12:17–21)

See the discussion under Session Two for information about how this type of session is to function.

Analysis:

The first question requires a certain amount of openness on the part of the group. If the group has developed a level of trust, this can be a most interesting discussion. Sometimes it is old grievances or feuds that inhibit our further growth. Identifying hostile relationships is the first step to healing.

Session Nine: Faith

See the discussion under Session One for information about how this type of session is to function.

Session Ten: Citizenship (Romans 13:1–7)

See the discussion under Session Two for information about how this type of session is to function.

Open:

Our views of government are often formed in childhood so this should be an interesting conversation. Question 3 may pose difficulties for some people who say "I have no authority over any one!" But this is probably not the case in that even at the level of the people we buy from or service people we employ, to some extent are beholden to us. Virtually everyone has some influence (power, authority) over someone else even if it is minimal.

Application:

Question 12 can be used if there is time. Since it deals with a situation different from our own it is possible to get at issues to which we might otherwise be blind.

Session Eleven: Community

See the discussion under Session One for information about how this type of session is to function.

LEADER'S NOTES FOR THIS STUDY

Session Twelve: Love in the Last Days (Romans 13:8–14)

General:

Since this is the final session in this small group series it is structured somewhat differently. The Open exercise is used as a way of summing up the small group experience and a Farewell section is added to the Prayer exercise at the end. Be aware of the times for each section. These are somewhat different than other even-numbered exercises.

Open:

This exercise asks people to reflect on their experience together during the weeks of the small group. Specifically, it asks people to reflect on what they have learned and experienced about transformation. It also asks people to sum up the good things that have happened in the small group.

Analysis:

This is a little briefer than normal.

Application:

- *Question 1*: The aim of this question is to help people see that law and love are not at odds but just different ways of approaching issues. Each is needed. Law gives shape to the substance of love; love provides the spirit in which law is lived out.

- *Question 2*: This is a powerful concept that enables people to do what they thought was possible, namely to love certain people whom they dislike. To understand love as not harming others gives one a good place to begin when it comes to difficult relationships.

- *Question 3*: This is the heart of the matter in which principles are located from the text and applied in real life. These are not idealistic maxims. They provide a concrete way to approach others. For example, the consciousness that Jesus may return today makes us alert to the need for love at all times in our relationships. The need to act in ways that we are happy for others to witness prevents us from brushing off our obligation to act in love to strangers in anonymous situations. Seeing love as not harming others makes it possible by what we do not do to act in love even to enemies. And the obligation to love others causes us to see other people differently. They are not objects of disregard, disdain, lust, pity, or any other attitude that is less than loving.

Farewell:

The aim of this exercise is to plan what is next as a group (if anything) and to have one final prayer experience together.

Bibliography

Appleton, George, ed. *Oxford Book of Prayer*. Oxford: Oxford University Press, 1985.
Augustine. *Confessions*. Translated by Henry Chadwick. 1991. Oxford: Oxford University Press, 1992.
Barclay, William. *The Letter to the Romans*. Edinburgh: Saint Andrew, 1955.
Barrett, C. K. *The Epistle to the Romans*. San Francisco: Harpers, 1957.
Bruce, F. F. *The Epistle of Paul to the Romans*. London: Tyndale, 1963.
Cranfield, C.E.B. *A Critical and Exegetical Commentary on the Epistle to the Romans* 2. Edinburgh: T. and T. Clark, 1979.
Jones, E. Stanley. *A Song of Ascents: A Spiritual Autobiography*. Nashville: Abington, 1968.
Menninger, Karl. *Whatever Became of Sin?* New York: Hawthorn, 1973.
Peace, Richard. *Contemplative Bible Reading: Experiencing God Through Scripture*. Eugene, OR: Wipf and Stock, 2015.
———. *Conversion in the New Testament: Paul and the Twelve*. Grand Rapids: Eerdmans, 1999.
———. *Meditative Prayer: Entering God's Presence*. Eugene, OR: Wipf and Stock, 2015.
———. *Noticing God*. Downers Grove, IL: InterVarsity, 2012.
———. *Pilgrimage: A Handbook on Christian Growth*. Grand Rapids: Baker, 1984.
———. *Spiritual Autobiography: Discovering and Sharing Your Spiritual Story*. Colorado Springs, CO: NavPress, 1998.
———. *Spiritual Journaling: Recording Your Journey Toward God*. Colorado Springs, CO: NavPress, 1998.
———. *12 Steps: The Path to Wholeness*. Colorado Springs, CO: Serendipity, 1990.
Peace, Richard and Lyman Coleman. *Pastor/Teacher Commentary for Romans*. Littleton, CO: Serendipity, 1986.
———. *Study Guide for the Book of Romans*. Littleton, CO: Serendipity, 1986.
Phinney Baskette, Molly. *Standing Naked Before God: The Art of Public Confession*. Cleveland: Pilgrim, 2015.
Robinson, John A. T. *Wrestling with Romans*. Louisville: Westminster, 1979.
Stott, John. *Romans: God's Good News for the World*. Downers Grove, IL: InterVarsity, 1995.
———. *Men Made New*. Grand Rapids: Baker, 1984.
Wagner, C. Peter. *Your Spiritual Gifts Can Help Your Church Grow*. Ventura, CA: Regal, 1982.

www.ingramcontent.com/pod-product-compliance
Lightning Source LLC
Chambersburg PA
CBHW060820190426
43197CB00038B/2171